Horses and Horse Shows

Also by Harlan C. Abbey: *Showing Your Horse*

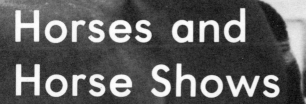

Horses and
Horse Shows

Harlan C. Abbey

South Brunswick and New York: A. S. Barnes and Company
London: Thomas Yoseloff Ltd

© 1980 A. S. Barnes and Co., Inc.

A. S. Barnes and Co., Inc.
Cranbury, New Jersey 08512

Thomas Yoseloff Ltd
Magdalen House
136-148 Tooley Street
London SE1 2TT, England

Library of Congress Cataloging in Publication Data

Abbey, Harlan C.
    Horses and horse shows

    1. Horse-shows. 2. Show riding. 3. Horses—
Showing. 4. Horse-training.   I. Title.
SF294.5.A2   798'.23   78-55449
ISBN 0-498-02247-1

Title page illustration:
It's nice to get into the habit of winning at an early age. This happy young lady has just won a pony hunter class at the Ox Ridge Horse Show. *Photo by Sue Maynard.*

PRINTED IN THE UNITED STATES OF AMERICA

to Gretel

Contents

Foreword

I have been involved in horse showing for a number of years, and have seen it grow from a small, socially oriented sport to one of the fastest-growing sports in North America for people from all walks of life.

Gone are the days of the horse for work; here are the days of the horse for pleasure and sport. He is found everywhere, from the back yard to the football stadium.

During the last decade I have been continually amazed that, despite periodic wars, political upheavals, unpredictable weather conditions, and great jumps in inflation, this sport has grown at such a rapid pace and encompassed such a variety of people.

Why do horses have so much going for them? With the increase in recreation and leisure time, it is one of the few sports in which you can participate from the time you are eight to the time you are eighty. Not many sports can say that. Why, if you haven't made the first team in a college sport by the time you finish, there is very little likelihood that you will actively participate in that sport again. With over two-thirds of your life left to be lived, riding is a natural.

What a variety it provides! There are all types and breeds to choose from, and there are all kinds of ways to enjoy the horse—breeding, driving, trail riding, polo, rodeoing, hunting, and of course, showing. With this sport you will find that the more you learn, the more there is to learn. And the appeal—horses appeal to many people for a variety of reasons. Consequently, people from the high road and the low road come together in a perfect mix; this one common interest brings us all to the same level.

So my friend Harlan has written another book, with all sorts of food for thought. He is one of us, not because he is a top rider (by his own admission he isn't), but because he enjoys horses, horse shows, and horse people. On the following pages you will find a collection of interviews and anecdotes that Harlan has compiled over the last few years. They will certainly appeal to those who are mostly horse-show minded; they include conversations with your favorite show-ring personalities, who relate their experiences and their tricks of the trade.

Harlan has the ability to make what they say interesting and informative. Those who are tops in their specialty field make it sound so simple, as if good horse sense were just plain common sense.

In this book Harlan shows a great feel for his subjects—the horse, the show scene, and the horse-show personalities. For those of us that show and for those of you that just enjoy being around at the shows, you cannot help but pick up useful and interesting information to make your association with horses and showing more enjoyable. For isn't that what it's all about?

R. James Elder
Captain, Canadian Equestrian Team

Acknowledgments

No equestrian journalist can get very far unless he likes horses and enjoys writing about them, in almost equal measures. So I would like to take this opportunity to thank those who have encouraged both my riding and my writing over the years.

First, my parents, Bernard and Ethel Abbey, for fostering my love for horses at an early age by buying me all the new books by the late C. W. Anderson, and my uncles, Dave and Jerry Dickler.

Then, the many fine horsemen I have ridden with, including Sgt. Kim and Lt. Kim of the Seoul, Korea, Mounted Police unit, where I rode over fences for the first time, Herbert and Robert Woodington, the late Elton Bream, the late Charles Hawkes, John and Debbie Shaffner of Hurdle Hill Farm and Ed Lane, who helped me so much with my first horse, Stability ("Billy") and now with Idarullah ("Hope").

Among the many editors who've published my work and otherwise encouraged me I would like to thank Marie Lafrenz, Lorraine Vincent, and Matt Stander of *American Horseman,* Alexander Mackay-Smith and Peter Winants of *Chronicle of the Horse,* Keith and Eva Stevens of *Hoofs and Horns* in Australia, William Robertson of *Thoroughbred Record,* Bill Welch of the *New York Thoroughbred Breeder,* and Robert Naylor.

I would also like to thank all the reviewers who had so many nice things to say about my first book, *Showing Your Horse,* written with Rodney Jenkins, Dave Kelley, and George Morris, and all the horse lovers who purchased the book. I feel its success has proved the worth of having leading professional horsemen discuss their training, riding, and breeding philosophies through

11

the interview method. And I likewise appreciate the cooperation of the horsemen interviewed in this book.

Photographs add so much to a book about horses that it is almost impossible to think of writing one before you have secured the services of a photographer. I have been very fortunate to have had the talents of Sue Maynard, Ken Schmidt, Robert A. Heinold, and Esther Peachey, as well as the other photographers whose work was loaned to me by my subjects.

My wife, Gretel, has waited many, many months for this book to be finished, and perhaps it never would have been without her verbal spurring. She always stopped short of drawing blood, fortunately.

Finally, I have to especially thank Thomas and Julien Yoseloff of A. S. Barnes and Co., Inc., my publishers, for their confidence in me since the idea for *Showing Your Horse* was submitted to them in a bare outline some ten years ago.

Horses and Horse Shows

1 Should I Enter My Horse in a Show?

Should I enter my horse in a show?

That question must enter the minds of hundreds of horse show spectators each year. Even if they aren't lucky enough to own a horse, they probably ask themselves that question. And why not? Spectators see other riders in equitation classes perform at the walk, trot or jog, and canter or lope, or over some low fences. "I can do that," they tell themselves. Or they see riders competing in classes where their horses perform the walk, trot or jog and canter/lope routine and say "My horse can do that" to themselves.

But it's not quite that simple. Yes, most riders can sit properly at the three basic gaits—but can they do it when their horse is feeling skittish because of other horses in the ring, with spectators leaning over the ring's top rail, and with music playing over the loudspeaker? Can they remember to keep their heads up and heels down while—in their minds—hundreds of pairs of eyes are scrutinizing their body position from hat to boot heels? The routine in most horse show classes, when you analyze it, really isn't too difficult. Neither is sinking a basket when no one is guarding the shooter.

There is a vast difference between riding through fields and woods having fun and performing in a ring before a judge. And while any horse with four sound legs and a manageable temperament fills the bill as a pleasure horse, the requirements for a successful show horse are much more demanding. This doesn't mean you can't compete in a show on a horse with serious conformation faults. It just means your chances of winning a ribbon on that horse are lessened to a great degree.

Unless you keep your horse at a stable that regularly sponsors

There are big horse shows—like Devon, Pennsylvania, where truly "champions meet." Bernie Traurig is shown riding Royal Blue in a hunter class. *Photo by Sue Maynard.*

Team roping can be just as competitive, even though it attracts far fewer spectators.

horse shows, or at one near enough so you can ride your horse to the show ring, entering a horse show can lead to considerable expense. If you don't own a trailer you'll have to pay for transportation in addition to entry fees. You might have to buy new equipment for your horse or yourself to meet the requirements of a class in which you plan to compete. You may have to rent a stall for your horse to stay in for the duration of the show. If the show is a considerable distance away you might have to stay overnight at a motel and eat several meals in restaurants.

So, before committing yourself (or your parents) to all that expense, it might be best to take a long, hard look at yourself and your horse in an imaginary mirror. Yes, you can stay in the saddle at the three basic gaits in the ring—but is your riding form good enough to gain a second look from a judge? Yes, your horse can perform all three gaits at your command—but can he perform the regular and extended trot that a road hack class calls for? In other

Maybe the young show rider can even wind up on the United States Equestrian Team, and someday replace (from left) Frank Chapot or Michael Matz or Buddy Brown or Dennis Murphy, shown here after winning the Prize of Nations competition in Madison Square Garden in 1976. *Photo by Sue Maynard.*

17

Or win a championship at halter at a national breed show, like the 1976 Appaloosa World Championship Show in Oklahoma City.

words, do you want to go and contribute your entry fees just to say you competed in the show, or do you want to give yourself and your horse a chance to come home with a ribbon?

The chances are that you will come to the same decision that I did many years ago, before I owned my first horse. Why not give it a try, I told myself; why not enter a show (on someone else's horse), do my best, and maybe surprise myself—and my friends— by winning a ribbon? Astonishingly enough, I did win two (fourth place) ribbons in my first show. Maybe you will, too.

I think the urge to compete is something common to most Americans. Our most popular team and individual sports are based on someone being better at something than someone else, at performing better at a specific time and date. Why should riding be any different? Didn't the "My horse is faster than your horse" syndrome lead ancient men to stage the first horse race, and later horse lovers to race over fences to a distant church steeple?

Nevertheless, however much you hope to spring a surprise on the other competitors, you have to realize that horse shows on every level—from strictly local affairs to huge international events—are very competitive. You should enter with the idea of performing as well as you can, making allowance for the show "nerves" every novice competitor is bound to experience, and nothing more. If the judge seems to take a good long look at you while you're performing, you should be satisfied. If you win a ribbon, it's the frosting on top of the cake.

If you have been analyzing your prospective competition at near-by shows you already should have figured out in which classes you and your horse will have the best chance. But if you can't, perhaps you should have a more experienced horseman play the part of the imaginary mirror. Demonstrate your skills before him (or her) and ask his honest opinion about your ability and potential in regard to showing, or a specific show.

In general, if your horse isn't good looking enough or doesn't move well enough to catch the judge's eye at the basic gaits, it might be better to concentrate on equitation classes. But if your form in the saddle has serious flaws that can't be corrected before the day of the show, you'd better stick to a performance class

But first you've got to start out with lots and lots of low fences, like this one being taken by Jennifer Elden, ten, and her good hunter pony, Teddy Rosshire. *Courtesy t. h. e. Studio; photo by Ken Schmidt.*

Yet no matter how much you practice and how many ribbons you have won, occasionally you're going to wind up looking like this! *Photo by Sue Maynard.*

your horse can handle, at least for your first show ring exposure.

You probably ought to allow at least three weeks to prepare for your first show, depending on the previous show experience of your horse or his ability to perform the class requirements. You need to study the class rules so you will know what is required, what clothing you must wear, and what equipment your horse must carry. You should obtain, or borrow, the rule book of the American Horse Shows Association, which covers most types of show classes. Even shows that are not recognized by the AHSA generally follow the AHSA rule book.

If your horse has to be transported to the show and hasn't been in a trailer lately—or ever—you've got to train him for that, as well as for the show. If you have been riding your horse with a martingale or tie-down and want to show him in a hack or pleasure class, he'll have to get familiar with being ridden without one. Many Western classes require the saddle to be equipped with a lariat and slicker—get your horse used to them.

Obviously, you've got to spend more time grooming your horse once you decide you're going to a show. And since you'll probably be riding him more regularly than before, and perhaps riding him harder, he'll probably need an increase in his daily feed, too.

Once your horse begins performing the class routine well at home, it's time to get him introduced to show ring conditions. Start playing a radio—loudly—at ringside when you ride him. Try to get some friends to ride with you, to familiarize him with working in a ring with strange horses. Take your horse to a friend's ring and work him there, to get him used to new conditions. Have friends line the ring, shouting and waving, perhaps holding balloons.

If your horse and you can perform correctly under these conditions, then you can be a little more confident when you actually enter your first show class. Good luck to the two of you.

On the following pages you will meet some of the nation's top professional and amateur horsemen, those who have achieved many successes in North America's major horse shows. They will discuss their show training techniques and philosophies. Hopefully their advice will speed your progress to a blue ribbon. Other material will deal with horse shows and some of the problems they present, some of my own ideas and personal experiences, and how one might go about becoming a professional horseman—and spend his next twenty or thirty years traveling to horse shows, if he's lucky.

2 Jimmy Williams: Training Techniques and Cowboy Psychology

In nearly forty years of training and riding horses, Californian Jimmy Williams has done it all—trained champion hunters, jumpers, stock horses, and pleasure horses; been a cowboy, then a stunt rider in movies; studied dressage in Europe; and trained champions in forward, stock, and saddle seat equitation.

The riding master of the Flintridge Riding Club in Pasadena through the years has developed his own style of "cowboy psychology" that has proved itself through the many successes of his two- and four-legged pupils. Surprisingly, especially for one whose early experience was in the rough-and-ready school, Williams objects to the time-honored phrase used by horsemen for so many years: "punishment and reward."

"I believe in reward, but I don't like the term *punishment* at all," Williams emphasizes. "To me punishment only leads to resentment in the horse. When the horse is resentful, you have another problem to overcome. So I prefer to avoid anything that even seems like punishment." Williams prefers the term *irritation* as a method of keeping the horse alert and responsive to the rider, explaining:

"I don't have to use a stick or a spur in a punishing way to get the horse to pay attention to me. You can 'tickle' him and get him to pay attention. I can pinch you, or just rub your cheek continually, and you'll pay attention. It's the same way with a horse. I can use a fingernail or just the tip of a dull nail, or just a little mild pressure with a spur.

"You want to stimulate a response, but never hurt the horse,

22

Veteran California horseman Jimmy Williams riding the good conformation hunter Gemini. At one time Williams served as the stunt "double" for movie star Tyrone Power.

never let him carry a grudge. When you're in the saddle, you're in charge. The horse is your slave. But you can't be sitting there with your mind in 'neutral.' First you've got to get his attention, through irritation if necessary. Heck, you wouldn't start a conversation with someone who was asleep in a chair would you? First you'd wake him up. Training a horse is the same thing."

Williams also disapproves of the use of the bitting rig, calling it "The worst single item of equipment you can use. There is no reward to it. The horse ends the punishment by pulling his head in but there is no reward for him. And how can you get him to reach out again and accept the bit? It's too mechanical for me.

"It's the same thing with many types of bits and much other equipment. Any well-broke hunter should be able to be ridden in a snaffle of some type. I think martingales, draw reins, and side reins are useless. They are the result of bad hands and bad legs and

Francie Steinwedell, a Jimmy Williams pupil, being awarded the trophy for winning the American Society for the Prevention of Cruelty to Animals (Maclay) championship for equitation at the 1977 National Horse Show in Madison Square Garden. Francie's mount is Hot Soup. *Photo by Sue Maynard.*

badly trained horses. Of course, even if the rider is applying his aids perfectly the horse could have a weakness or problem, so at times you are forced to use them."

For a former cowboy, Williams is unusual in his preference for the Thoroughbred. He rode many in Western classes before World War II and uses them exclusively as hunters and jumpers. "The Thoroughbred is the best horse in the world," he asserts. "All the good Quarter Horses that I've seen are three-fourths to seven-eighths Thoroughbreds.

"I buy most of my horses at the racetrack, and prefer it that way. I'd rather have a horse that has raced, or at least galloped, because he has been taught how to extend and lengthen his stride. And I have found no difference in temperament between those which have raced and those which haven't. A horse can learn bad habits anywhere, especially in the backyard as a pet.

"I teach my young horses basic dressage. Not many trainers like that term, *dressage,* but if they are turning out a horse that is well trained on the flat they are doing dressage training, whether they call it that or not. The shoulder-in, being the only basic dressage movement where the horse is *not* looking in the direction he is going in, is the most helpful (used only as an exercise).

"After I get a horse moving forward and accepting the bridle, I start my collection, transferring the weight from the forehand to the haunch. My aim is to make them into athletes, stretch them out and compress them in like a rubber band. Later on you can loosen up and let the horse move in the more natural-looking way, the prettiest, most perfect way for him to travel. When I am working a horse on the basics, he works seven days a week. If you never let them rest a day, then they never get an inch ahead of you. After this intense period they are rewarded by a time of relaxation, such as trail rides or spending the day in a paddock.

"My approach to training a horse—and a rider—is to build up his confidence, let him think he can jump over the Empire State Building. I don't want him to learn what he cannot do. For that reason I don't like solid fences, or telephone poles used as cavalletti. They can hurt a horse. And you can't limit the horse's

Jimmy Williams's jumping chute. The outside length measures 150 feet and the inside is 100 feet. He can put seven "no stride" jumps down each side, twelve feet apart. The lanes are twelve feet wide and the space on the turns measures twenty-four feet wide.

progress by being stupid, by doing the same thing the same way to every horse."

Williams has raised a large number of horses over the years, and here, too, his methods go against the accepted. "It may shock a lot of people, but I have taught a lot of colts to jump while they were still nursing, at three to six months of age," he asserts. "Many horsemen think this is all wrong, but I think the foals I've started this way have turned out to be good jumpers.

"The point I'd like to emphasize is that foals' legs are almost as long as they'll be at five years of age, but the distance from the point of the shoulder to the top of the wither isn't more than twelve to fourteen inches. This means the foals can't have very much weight to lift on those long legs, so they can fold up and raise their knees and develop that classy look I like them to have.

"Another proof of this method are the pony hunters and pony jumpers. They all use themselves so well and fold up so well that people always ask 'Why can't my horse jump like that pony?' The reason they jump so well is that they have nothing much in the way of their own weight and that of their riders to lift. I think this method does not break a horse down and it does make good jumpers."

An essential part of Jimmy Williams's training program is the use of a Hitchcock jumping pen, although the veteran horseman points out, "It's so easy to ruin a horse in a jumping pen." The "secret," he insists, is to have one that is rectangular in shape, built solid only up to four feet in height. The rest is made by two-by-sixes built to eight feet in height so the horse *can* see out. The trainer must ride the horse in it before he is ever turned loose.

Williams's pen is one hundred fifty feet overall in length, forty-eight feet in width, and the lanes are twelve feet wide on the sides and twenty-four feet wide on the ends. The inside of the pen is one hundred feet in length and twenty-four feet in width. He uses this inside area for schooling young horses and riders. The four corners force a horse to slow down and prevent him from getting too quick.

"Not many other horsemen seem to believe in the rectangular-shaped pen," Williams contends. "They all want oblong ones with rounded turns. The reason I don't like rounded turns is that I've seen many horses hurt in them. The fence is always curving and coming to the horse. Horses get to climbing the wall and hurting themselves, whereas going down the lane with square corners a

Jimmy Williams in the inside portion of his jumping chute, which is ideal for the aggressive horse. "I send them over two low jumps, thirty-six feet apart, leaving them only thirty-six feet in which to stop before coming to an eight-foot fence," he explains. "When he takes the second jump and sees the high fence, he slows down by himself."

horse will slow down his own pace; he'll round off the rest of the turn by himself—square corners are speed controllers.

"The secret is to ride them in it first. You use the corners to stop them and reverse them. I ride them in the pen, ride them over four-inch poles on the ground, teach them how to get around the pen. Then we let them go at liberty.

"You build the size of the fences according to the mentality of the individual horse, to keep his interest up. If he's handling the low verticles well, then we spread them out a bit, to develop that nice arc over a fence. Then you can raise them a little, if the horse accepts it. If he doesn't, don't raise them. But you don't want to bore him by putting him over low fences again and again, condemning him because of what a less-intelligent horse will accept. And I don't worry if he gets a little sloppy over his fences and try to correct him. A lot of nice horses get sloppy at one time or another, but time will improve them."

The pen is part of Williams's daily training routine for his young prospects, but it might be for only a fifteen-minute session and it

Williams's schooling pen has numbers in every corner. When his students ride in the pen he uses the numbers as focal points.

may not involve any jumping. "I use it like others use a longe line," says Williams. "After they go into the pen they go on the walker for an hour. This not only gets my horses fit, it also conditions my tough horses to where I can teach them something once I get on them."

Williams has won just about everything there is to win on the West Coast and has sent a good stream of talented equitation horses to the East, along with the fine jumper Icy Paws, ridden by Rodney Jenkins. Icy Paws was such a talented jumper that he soon won enough prize money to go from the preliminary to the intermediate division. That's when Williams decided to send him East, where the lower jumper divisions do not pay as much money, and where Icy Paws had more time to move into the open division in graduated steps.

A steady stream of equitation champions has come from the Flintridge Riding Club, too, headed by Mary Mairs (now Mrs. Frank Chapot), who was only the third rider to win the American Horse Shows Association's Medal championship and the American Society for the Prevention of Cruelty to Animals finals in the same year and later rode on the U. S. Equestrian Team (USET); Luann

The most important factor in using a jumping chute is the trainer's body position. Here Jimmy Williams is on the opposite side of the ring with his whip following the horse's hindquarters.

Beach, who won both the AHSA's saddle seat and stock seat Medal finals; Robert Ridland, a USET member who competed in the Montreal Olympics; Wendy Mairs, and Francie Steinwedel, who won the AHSA Medal finals in 1976. His top stock horses included Red Hawk, Henny Penny, Woodwind, and Champagne.

In addition to the awards won by the horses and riders he has trained, Williams has been cited by the Western Fairs Association and the American Humane Society and received a Patsy Award, similar to the Oscar, for the performance of the gray horse Alborado in the Walt Disney production of *The Horse in the Gray Flannel Suit*.

Williams emphasizes the "natural look" in teaching equitation. He points out that if a mounted rider lets his hands and arms hang loosely down at his sides and moves them to where he can hold the reins, they end up naturally slanted at a thirty-degree angle inside the verticle. This puts a rider's hands parallel to and conforming with the angle of a horse's shoulder.

"The wrist should be rounded to where you can just see your fingernails," he continues. "Your hands should be no farther apart than your thumbs—if you turn your hands so the knuckles are

29

Always stop the horse when he is in a corner, facing the trainer.

"After the horse has stopped, you should go out and pet him," Williams believes. "This reward keeps him from becoming frightened of you."

pointing forward—extended and touching. That is about four and a half inches, the natural width of a horse's mouth. And the hands should be no higher than the length of the thumbs—extended downward toward the horse's neck. The leg should be about four inches behind the girth. Putting it all together presents an artistically perfect picture, and a good rider is—I feel—an artist. The perfect picture, however, can only take place on a well-schooled horse. Otherwise, you have to make minor adjustments.

"To develop my rider's posture, I give my pupils a preparatory command, and then ask them to execute it as I give the old cavalry command "Ho-oh!" When they hear the preparatory words, they should take a deep breath and then let half of it out. That gets the chest up and the loins hollow. This also gives them time to consciously organize their thoughts as to executing the proper aids. It forces them to think and condition their reflexes. When it comes to applying the aids I emphasize that you use your head before you use your hands or legs. You get the horse listening to you and paying attention first, then you tell him what to do."

Williams believes the sitting trot is the most important exercise for a rider to work at, because it forces him to sink lower and lower into the saddle. This develops the rider's feel of a horse. He also has his riders count the beat of the horse's stride out loud. This helps to coordinate their voice, and body rhythm, to the horse's stride.

During one of his rare clinics conducted in the East, Williams conducted a majority of jumping exercises on a broken line. This forces the rider to use his lateral and diagonal aids more effectively. Another exercise used here was the half-stop, an example of which is a decrease in the speed of the trot from eight miles per hour to six miles.

"To develop both horse and rider you want to work at lots of half-stops and transitions from gait to gait," he continued. "We want to stretch the horse out like a rubber band, to make him more flexible and responsive, then compress him like a spring. The proper timing and use of the aids is so important. When working green horses on a track to the right, for example, the smoothest way to push him from the walk into the canter is to use your left leg, with a supporting right leg, as the horse's left shoulder is coming back. I teach my beginner riders to first watch, then feel for that shoulder to come back. This develops their timing for a smooth and polished transition from the walk into the canter.

31

Robert Ridland, a Jimmy Williams-trained rider, competing on the USET's Almost Persuaded at the Lake Placid, New York, Horse Show in 1976. *Photo by Sue Maynard.*

Jimmy Williams and his top assistant, Susan Hutchison, schooling Anne Kursinki prior to a horse show class.

"To be coherent with a horse's forward motion, you should close the angles—elbows, hips, knees, and ankles—in relation to the rate of speed at which you are traveling. The faster the rate of speed, the more the angles are closed; the slower the rate of speed, the more open. To be coherent while riding a curve you sit a little deeper on the inside seat bone, returning to both seat bones when you reach the straightaways. On a curve, the arc of the horse should be the same as the arc of the curve, which again is achieved by the use of diagonal aids.

"To move a horse forward I tell my students, 'You drive from your leg and seat bones, don't lead with your nose.' If their head is too far forward, the horse, who should be the slave, is in command—instead of the master. And when you have to stop your horse, you can get your feet a little bit in front of the girth and brace against them. But once the horse stops, you quickly get those feet back where they belong."

Jimmy Williams, although describing the rider as "master" and the horse as "slave," believes the most common mistake he sees is the rider "telling" the horse when to jump, instead of "waiting" for the horse to jump. "He's your slave, yes," he explains, "but you have to tell him way before the jump, not on the last stride. The last stride is where the anxiety arises, and that's why I want to draw my riders' attention to a spot at least thirty feet in front of the jump, giving them two strides or more to get right.

"Developing a good eye for the approach is not only important in developing a good rider, it also is a safety factor," Williams stresses. "If you are able to develop your ability to ride in rhythm to the horse's stride and see your strides to the various fences, then you'll always know where you are."

Williams's favorite exercise for developing a rider's "eye for a fence" is to use a small oxer and three numbered markers on the ground, in a line perpendicular and to the side of the fence. "I place marker No. 1 at a measured distance of thirty feet away from the fence, then I measure twelve feet from that marker, toward the jump and place my No. 2 marker, then I measure another twelve feet closer to the jump and place the No. 3 marker, leaving a six-foot takeoff (assuming they are going twelve miles per hour, 360 yards a minute, a perfect hunter pace for this exercise). However, if the stride carries you beyond the first marker you should retard slightly and wait for the jump to occur. If you land in front of the first marker, you may have to lengthen the horse's

Jimmy Williams riding Gemini at the Diamond Bar National Horse Show in California. Gemini won Pacific Coast point championships in both 1971 and 1972.

stride. This exercise takes away the last-minute anxiety most riders feel directly in front of the jump.

"I also ask the rider to count out loud 'one' when he feels the horse complete his last stride before takeoff in front of the fence. After he does that a couple of times I ask him to count 'one' 'two' in front of the fence, then 'one' 'two' 'three', 'one' 'two' 'three' 'four', and finally have them counting up to five. This is a wonderful exercise to develop an 'eye.' It gets you used to 'dancing' with the horse, working as a pair. But, if you can't do it consistently over low fences, you'll never be a consistent rider over higher fences."

One of the riders in the clinic was having a problem with her horse getting too strong approaching the low parallel. Williams advised her: "Don't let your legs, working through the horse's hind legs, and your weight on his back, keep driving him crazy. Take a shorter hold, lighten your seat, close the angles, and let your hands work through his mouth for a while." Williams then had the rider circle her horse at one end of the arena, opening and closing her body angles (doing an exercise called the "one-two," which is like posting at the canter) and also running one hand up along the neck to stroke the horse and calm him. He then went back to jumping in a more relaxed manner, and Williams had the rider keep the angles closed for two more counts after jumping, which kept the horse relaxed and made the entire process smoother. "Weight influence used properly is an asset; used improperly it is a detriment," he pointed out.

Williams feels the reason most horses refuse to jump a fence is that the rider "drops him" right before a fence—loses contact with the horse's mouth by dropping the reins or loosening them to place his hands on the horse's neck. However, an experienced rider, with an educated leg, can get by with dropping a horse anywhere.

"I tell my riders, 'If you are going to drop him before the fence, you may as well dig a hole for him there,' " he joked. "That will make them think a bit. Usually they are dropping the horse because they are looking down at the fence. They have to learn to practice focusing on something beyond the fence that is level with their eyes."

A California native who began her career with Jimmy Williams, Francie Steinwedell came East to compete with distinction. She is shown riding Hot Soup at Lake Placid. *Photo by Sue Maynard.*

The Flintridge Riding Club riding master, Jimmy Williams, and his assistants frequently take as many as seventy-five horses and riders to the big California shows. How can he keep a "happy ship" with so many riders from the same stable competing against one another? "I teach the parents as we go along," he replied. "I have a portable loudspeaker on my golf cart and when I'm instructing they all hear what I say. I make them smart. I drum it into their ears. Then they become better sports and aren't so quick to criticize or condemn their children. They learn to appreciate what their children are learning, and this eliminates most of the friction.

"I would say the top level of horsemanship in California is as good as there is anywhere in the country. Our top ten percent are fine riders. But, there are so many more hunter-jumper riders in the East, and so many more knowledgeable trainers for them to work under, that the overall depth of talent is much greater there.

Probably Jimmy Williams's most famous pupil was Mary Mairs Chapot, who competed with distinction with the United States Equestrian Team and married fellow team member Frank Chapot. Mary is shown competing on Good News, a son of the Olympic jumper Good Twist, at the Ox Ridge Show. *Photo by Sue Maynard.*

"Showing in any part of the country is very competitive. If a horse hasn't any natural talent—can't use his shoulder and head and neck—I can't do much for him. I can only give him confidence and make him want to jump. I start out about fifteen young ones a year. If I find two or three that can compete at A-rated shows, I think I'm doing very well. If I can get one consistent winner every year or two, I'm doing great."

3 John Shaffner:
Analyzing Equine Personality Types

There are four distinct types of horse personalities, according to professional trainer John Shaffner, and each requires special adjustments to make the training process run as smoothly as possible. Yet neither the horse's personality nor the trainer's philosophy is as important as a trainer's powers of observation, which should enable him to adjust every training session to the horse's physical and mental state, which can change greatly from day to day.

"I don't think you can approach a training session with a particular horse," the owner of Hurdle Hill Farm in Lockport, New York, explains, "with a preconceived idea of what you will do. So much depends on how the horse looks and acts when he comes out of his stall.

"Does he look tired? Maybe he should get a day off, just be turned out rather than ridden. Does he seem a little stiff or sore—not sore enough to nod and be lame, but you just see 'a little something?' Then you have to give him less work than you might have thought he needed.

"Sometimes—almost always with a young horse—he should be turned out or longed first, then ridden. Some you might have to turn out a second time and then ride again later in the day. Sometimes you turn a horse out, then groom him, then ride him. I believe a horse should be happy in his work, and you can see he's unhappy when he's moving 'short' in front or behind. Is he pinning his ears or shaking his head? Maybe the rider is confining him too much, giving him too much slow, regimented work.

John Shaffner, one of the East's leading hunter-jumper trainers, believes the horseman's powers of observation are the key to proper training. *Courtesy t. h. e. Studio; photo by Ken Schmidt.*

"Is he landing after a fence with his ears pinned back? Something's obviously wrong, and you'd better figure out—quickly—what it is. It's all in your eyes and brain. It's impossible to keep notes. You develop a method of training through time and experience and from those horses you've ruined—and we've all done it. The more horses you are around and observe on a daily basis, the better your powers of observation will become and the better a trainer you'll be."

Among the horses Shaffner has trained or has handled in more than twenty years as a professional are such well-known ribbon-winners as Nemesis, Columbia, Market Rise, Another Legend, Miss December, Chili Multi, Bakerstown, Nevermore, Vintage Year, Big

Decision, Computer, Stash the Cash, Mr. Sandman, More, Altar Boy, Sparkle, Clouds, Eddie Eastman, and Alezan. He rode regularly on the "A" show circuit until about five years ago, when his wife, the former Debbie Hecht of Syracuse, took over the reins and Shaffner began concentrating on training from the ground.

The four personality types he classifies most horses into are: bold, tense, too quiet, and timid. The characteristics are as follows: The bold horse is no problem, as long as you don't ask him to do impossible things. If he does what you want boldly, it's fine, there's no problem. In time he'll learn how to put in a short stride and not let his boldness get him into trouble. The problems usually arise when a poor rider gets the horse into trouble.

The overly quiet horse usually is a very young horse who doesn't know much and is not really paying much attention to his rider. This is the horse that especially should not be rushed. As he is worked more and asked to do more, he will "wake up" and pay more attention.

The tense horse is the hardest to work with and the hardest to

John and Debbie Shaffner at the entrance to Hurdle Hill Farm in Lockport, New York. *Courtesy t. h. e. Studio; photo by Ken Schmidt.*

figure out how to train. The horse can be tense no matter what rider is on him, so the condition can't be blamed on the rider. This horse can't be ridden as much, or as aggressively, as the other personality types. He must be trained slowly and gradually, with lots of even, slow work. This horse must be turned out frequently, perhaps all night the day before he's to show. And the condition does not depend on whether a Thoroughbred (for instance) has been raced or not. "Some horses have never been on the track and are twice as tense as those which have raced for a couple of years," he points out.

The fourth type of equine personality is the timid horse. Whereas the tense horse is always ready, always chomping on the bit, the timid horse is backwards, behind the bit, hanging back, being a bit "chicken." He's not spooky, but he doesn't want to do things. He's resentful. This horse you spend more time with, but he needs a lot more work across country than inside a ring or arena. He has to be shown more new sights to get him interested in his "lessons."

"It's impossible to do too much flat work with a horse,"

Debbie Shaffner exercising Sue Cox's At Last, a green working hunter who won five championships in 1977. "At Last is an extremely good mover," says Debbie's husband, John, "and here she is extending due to the use of the rider's seat—but Debbie's feet have slipped forward a little." *Courtesy t. h. e. Studio; photo by Ken Schmidt.*

Shaffner contends, "but it's very easy to do too much jumping. Most horses are jumped too much. It's not that it's so much harder physically—but overjumping leads to them getting sloppy, rubbing fences, and picking up bad habits through getting tired. I feel a horse has only so many really good jumps in him. Why not save them for when they count instead of wasting them showing the horse off for his owner, or the trainer's girl friend? This is supposed to be a show horse, so save him for the shows."

Shaffner picks his show prospects on the basis of "size, movement, and quality" and feels very few non-Thoroughbreds have the quality necessary to win in today's top show rings. When it comes to size, it's the horse of sixteen hands or over who fits more riders, "just like most pants are in the thirty-two- to thirty-six-inch waist sizes," he added. "Some horses are just too small. A quiet Thoroughbred that's 15.1 I wouldn't even go to look at, no matter what its price.

"I don't think you save anything by buying a cheap yearling at auction. If you add two years of feeding or boarding there's very little savings compared to buying a horse that's two and a half years old or three years old that you can see has the size to make it and can show some athletic ability over a fence. Many horsemen take a string and measure a yearling from his elbow to his fetlock, then pivot the string around the other way; where the top of the string ends up is how high the colt's withers will be at maturity. But it's not always a matter of inches. You have to know horses, or know a particular horse's breeding.

"When it comes to buying a horse, that is the cheapest part of it. The board is the same for a 'prospect' or a 'made' horse. The feed, the trucking, the lessons all cost the same. So why not buy a horse that will do the job for someone who wants to show him? The prospect or green horse is for the professional or for someone who doesn't want to show for a year or so.

"I would prefer not to buy a horse off the racetrack. I, personally, haven't had that much success with those I've started right from the track. Yet many of my older show horses are tattooed, so they must have raced at some time. But I didn't start those horses. I prefer to buy from breeders.

"Age is not that much of a factor any more. A few years ago a twelve-year-old was ready to go to a camp. Now they are taken care of so much better that a twelve-year-old can go on and show for several years. It all depends on his health. If he's in good

Debbie Shaffner and Another Legend competing at the Chagrin Falls, Ohio, Horse Show in 1977. During the season this pair won six championships and eight reserves, mainly in open conformation hunter divisions. *Photo by Sue Maynard.*

condition, is healthy, and can do the job in the show ring, age means nothing."

"I want a horse that travels true and straight, using his shoulders and not just flipping his legs. I want him to use his whole body. The quality has to be through the whole horse, not just his head or his tail. It's the individual's taste and what he thinks a quality horse should be. That's why the conformation hunter division often is so hard to figure out. What you can live with some judges can't.

"A little curb or splint can go right down, but it seems like the judges want clean legs above everything else. I don't agree with this one hundred percent. I've never seen a curb, for instance, hurt a horse's jumping form and I'd hate to pin a horse with one below an ugly-headed horse, as I often see done by some judges. Sure, I like a horse with a nice head—but I have to admit I don't spend a lot of time looking at a horse's head when I'm deciding whether or not to buy him. They still have to get over those 'sticks' and do it right; if they can move and jump, that's what it takes to win."

Shaffner also wants to watch the prospective show horse jump something, even if it's only cross rails. "If they use their legs and body right from the start, it's a lot easier," he maintains. "You want to see him curl up his front legs—pick up the knees and bring the forelegs back under them, not just let them hang down. They've got to bend at their joints—the neck, shoulders, back—and use their whole bodies, just not one or two parts.

"Even if a horse is a great mover and shows great athletic ability over fences there is no way you can be one hundred percent sure he will make a show horse. There can be a million problems, most of them relating to temperament. The horse can be great at home and go to a show and not accept the crowd or a strange ring—or won't jump out of a sand ring—or go into strange stalls."

Shaffner starts out a youngster with a bitting rig, just to get the colt to mouth it. He'll be longed in the bitting rig and driven from

At Last "is a bit too much on her front end," according to John Shaffner. "If you look at her overall silhouette, you can see that she seems to be going 'downhill,' so to speak. Another indication is that the mare's mouth is open." *Courtesy t. h. e. Studio; photo by Ken Schmidt.*

44

the ground later. This is all to teach the horse obedience and manners. All the trainer is aiming for at this stage is to get the horse to walk, trot, and stop.

"I'll always start a colt in my indoor ring," he explains. "Usually I'm starting them late in the year, but even if it's summer it is better that the youngster is confined. If something happens and he throws the rider and gets away, he can't get hurt if he's in an indoor ring. It's all walk and trot when they are first ridden, walk and trot. They get more balance that way. After a while, they will automatically break into a canter, sort of 'fall' into it. You don't let them canter too much when they first do it. But it shows you they are ready to go on and do more, and then they will get more work—circles, serpentines, and so on. If a horse needs to be pushed into a canter we usually do it from a collected trot and by using the inside aides. But mostly it's walk and trot, bending on the circles, and bending the entire body through the use of the rider's aids.

"I've always felt strongly that a colt has to be well broke, be balanced, and have good manners before he's ready to start jumping. He needs all that just to be a good horse. I consider walking, trotting, and cantering over poles work on the flat, not jumping. Sometimes I put one rail on top of another to give him something a little more 'formal,' to make him step out, think a little more, pay attention.

"I prefer to do most of the training with a rider on a horse's back; it has simply worked out well for me. I will longe a horse over a few cross rails just to get him used to the idea of jumping, or I might make a temporary jumping chute in my indoor arena and let a horse go up and down that a few times—but not to any great extent.

"By the time a horse is well broke on the flat, doing a slow and extended trot and a quiet canter—no extended canter or hand galloping just yet—then he is ready to trot over cross rails, then a very little vertical of one-and-a-half or two feet. How does he handle it? Is he using himself properly? You want to develop form as you develop ability.

"If you go slow enough you won't have any problems. If the horse is well broke on the flat there is no reason for him to become a 'maniac' when it comes to jumping." Later Shaffner has the young hunter go over little oxers, then a couple of cross rails sixty to seventy-two feet apart, and then a couple of small

45

John and Debbie Shaffner discussing a practice fence at Hurdle Hill Farm. Debbie is riding Neal Shapiro's Jason. *Courtesy t. h. e. Studio; photo by Ken Schmidt.*

verticals the same distance apart. After that it's feeling and observing what the horse is accepting, and what he is ready to go on to.

When it comes to problems that develop in jumping style—not using the neck, back, or legs, or twisting—John Shaffner believes

46

Leather Goods, a jumper owned by Dr. Howard Clement, just "hunting" over a fence for rider Debbie Shaffner at Hurdle Hill Farm. *Courtesy t. h. e. Studio; photo by Ken Schmidt.*

there can be more than one cure for each type of problem. Hanging legs or carelessness often is cured by "rapping" with a bamboo pole. "I don't use it," he points out "but someone else may have been poling for twenty years and producing winners—so how can you say he's wrong?

"The neck and back seem to work together, what corrects one will correct the other. I like to put a pole on the far side of the fence, on the ground. That makes the horse look at it when he's on the top of the fence, and forces him to use his head and neck, and also his back. Or you might place a pole twelve feet in front or twelve feet behind the fence, to accomplish the same thing.

"To make him use his front legs better you set up a gymnastics series, a row of little fences, some with one stride between and some with no strides. The last fence should be a square—the same height as it is wide—and two strides away from the fence before it. Or you might have the last two be little squares."

Shaffner believes dragging hind legs are easier to correct, again by using the square fence. The horse catches his hind legs a couple

47

Debbie Shaffner and Leather Goods soaring high over an oxer fence. *Courtesy t. h. e. Studio; photo by Ken Schmidt.*

of times on the second element of the fence and soon learns to tuck his legs for a little longer period of time. Hind leg problems are much less of a problem than those "up front."

Once a horse can handle a small in-and-out fence Shaffner moves him into gymnastics, lines of fences set up at varying distances from each other but in a straight line. These can be set for "long" or "short" strides to teach the horse to be supple and athletic, or at even distances. The "no stride" sequence is good, he believes, "because the horse has to hit the ground and leave right away. It teaches the horse to jump up 'around' the fence, not to jump in and leap straight out.

"But you have to analyze everything very carefully. A setup that works with one quiet horse might not 'wake up' the next one. A 'no-stride' does seem to make a horse a bit quicker, and should certainly not be used too often with a horse with a 'tense' personality.

"With a horse that rushes you'd generally make him halt on the approach. Having the first rail of a gymnastics series higher than the next should slow him down, too. If a horse throws his rear end, put a rail on the side where he is swinging out. They don't want to hit the rail, so they'll jump straighter. A horse finds he can jump a fence with less effort by twisting his hind end, so he does it. Try to catch it before it develops into a habit.

"You do find that many horses that move low to the ground and reach way out—good movers—usually do it just with their legs and not with their shoulders when they begin jumping. You can't really change their natural style too much, so you simply try to improve them enough to look decent. Gymnastic exercises will help some, as will square fences wider than normal. A wire across the top of some cross rails will sting and teach the horse to lift his legs higher.

"Refusals can result from many causes. The horse can be frightened, distracted, or sore. If it's not that, it's probably the rider. Many riders move up over the horse's neck too fast. I have to constantly emphasize to my riders not to get ahead of the horse with their upper bodies. The front feet have to come off the ground before the upper body moves. It's hard to learn. But if the

Leslee Clement schooling Columbia at Chagrin Falls. Judging from Columbia's expression, he's not too happy! *Photo by Sue Maynard.*

49

horse is stopping 'dirty' and it's not the rider's fault, the horse is going to have to be punished. I believe in using a stick behind the leg—and only using it once—most of the time."

Shaffner believes a horse bucking while jumping "is not a bad thing. If they are 'on the level' about it and not being mean, it may just mean that jumping the fence felt good to them. You have to watch enough horses so you can learn what they are trying to tell you. It takes time. And if a horse does a gymnastics line, or a line of two fences on a hunter course, well three or four times, that's enough."

When it comes to working with junior riders, Shaffner believes there are built-in problems during the school year. "Usually one horse is as much as a child going to school has time for," he agreed, "but you have to be able to ride all types of horses to become a good rider. Lots of riders can win at 'A' shows on 'a' horse, one made horse. Put them up on five horses at a show a few

A relaxed and alert Leather Goods and Debbie Shaffner compete in a preliminary jumper class at the Lake Placid Horse Show. *Photo by Sue Maynard.*

times and the other four would confuse them so much they'd soon spoil their good 'made' horse. Some move long, some short, some medium. Some jump to the right or left, some twist a little. You have to have 'mileage' on all types to be a 'rider.' It's one thing to be able to ride 'a' horse, another thing to make even a school horse do it all correctly. When you can, then you have a shot at doing it on a good horse."

During the school year Shaffner schools his young riders on Wednesday nights. They work without stirrups for about a half-hour at the posting and extended trot, counter canter, and extended canter. Turns on the forehand and haunches and the shoulder in and shoulder out teach the horse to move away from

Another Legend and Debbie Shaffner getting ready to compete at Chagrin Falls. This combination won thirty classes during the 1977 show season, while Debbie's other mounts won another eighty-four classes. *Photo by Sue Maynard.*

the leg. Serpentines teach riders to use their eyes ahead and to the side. Sometimes a row of fences with wings are set up as riders go over them with their hands on their hips or on their heads, to stress proper leg position. Shaffner also works on teaching riders to count strides, and frequently has them ride a line of the indoor hunter course leaving out a stride one time, adding a stride the next time.

"Every rider has a basic, individualistic style," he believes. "Not all can look the same over a fence. Some have the same basic body build but ride differently. What you are trying to do is develop something in each rider that will catch the judge's eye and give him a chance to win an equitation class.

"Much of it is fitting them on a horse that will suit their build. A narrow-bellied horse, for instance, will make a shorter, stockier rider's legs look longer. If a child has extremely long legs you look for a round-barreled horse. Some riders have to bend a little more forward over a fence to cover up a stocky body and short arms. Some riders are better on a horse they don't have to push, because when they push their legs back a little they have a tendency to topple forward a bit. For those you want a horse that moves on. An easy-going, less-aggressive rider fits on an easy-going, long-striding horse. Pairing up horses and riders is an art in itself. But it's not as important to a trainer as the art of observing his horses and training them accordingly."

4 Michael Page:
How to Deal with Unusual Mentalities

When Michael Page was working toward his total of nine Olympic
and Pan American Games medals in the three-day event, he spent
nearly as much time in Europe as he did in his native New York.
After winning the American Horse Shows Association's Medal
horsemanship championship and the American Society for the
Prevention of Cruelty to Animals Maclay national finals in 1956,
he spent a summer in England with Capt. Edy Goldman. Later he
completed the sixteen-month officer's training course at the
French Cavalry School at Saumur. He spent considerable time
riding in West Germany with Dr. Reiner Klimke, who later won an
Olympic gold in dressage. He also spent a summer in England with
noted eventing trainer Lars Sederholm, with whom he had
attended Saumur.

So you might think that when you sat down to talk horses and
horsemanship with Michael Page his conversation would be
somewhat beyond the comprehension of the average horseman,
and sprinkled with German, French, or British equestrian terms.
But, surprisingly, when Page discusses horsemanship and some of
the horse retraining projects he has undertaken, the terms are
those which even the novice rider can comprehend.

And when he teaches a clinic, which he does only once or twice
each year, you'll find him using the very same basic instructional
terms used by all other knowledgeable instructors—who may not
have his classical equitation background but still know that good
equitation position and proper control of the horse come from a
deep seat, strong leg, and soft upper body.

Michael Page, winner of nine Olympic and Pan American Games medals in the three-day event, talks things over with his wife during a training session. *Photo by Sue Maynard.*

"Basically," he contends, "my theory and principles of horsemanship are very simple; it is the execution of the basics that is difficult. The mechanics of riding a horse are simple, but the feeling and involvement with the horse become more and more complex as you get better. The horse and his specific problems and the rider and his problems are two separate entities. Fusing and joining the two, physically and mentally, into one unit is the instructor's problem.

"But what you must accept, no matter what your riding experience, is that most problems that arise are not complex. They really are very simple. Let's face it, both the Olympic rider and the cross-rail beginner have the same basic problem: getting the horse over the obstacle.

"I feel any mistake the horse makes is traceable to a mistake made by the rider in the application of his aids, or the independent use of them. This is what we start with, the proper position leading to the independent seat and the independent use of the aids, thus giving the rider the best chance to communicate with the animal. Once you have the rider riding correctly, then you can work on improving the animal through the proper application of the aids.

"The basic equitation position can best be improved through riding without stirrups, so as to get as deep into the horse as possible and get the maximum amount of the leg on the horse. So our aim is a firm, independent lower position, a steady, strong seat, enhanced by a soft upper body and a kind hand."

Page, individual Gold Medalist in the 1959 and 1963 Pan American Games, feels a stronger lower leg position is the most important factor in keeping the seat independent. The strong lower leg enables the rider to create impulsion, and encourages communication with the horse in a strong and simple manner. The

Michael Page working with Newton's Law, a young jumper he hopes may be capable of competing at the Moscow Olympic Games in 1980. *Photo by Sue Maynard.*

55

seat and legs create the energy that the hands direct, he believes, stating, "The motor is behind the rider. The legs create the power. The hands are the 'throttle' that allocate and then guide that power."

In dealing with problems that develop with the horse, Page believes in taking a step backwards to analyze what is creating the problem. "If you understand the basic mechanics of the equitation process," he said, "nine times out of ten you will find problems can be solved by going back to the basics—an independent seat and aids. And if the rider hasn't mastered them, he hasn't the ability to conquer the problems.

"Horses that rush their fences, I believe, do so because the rider is hanging onto their mouths and so they want to get the entire jumping process—and the pain—over with as swiftly as possible. To deal with the rushing problem, one must go back to the basics. If

Michael Page showing Singapore at the Lake Placid Horse Show in 1974. Later a Grand Prix jumper, Singapore is one of Page's most successful reclamation projects.

the rider works on strengthening his seat he will not have to hang on the horse's mouth. If the horse is made to trot his fences, through the use of cavalletti and combinations of fences set at the trotting stride, then he can't rush his fences. What you want to avoid is asking either the horse or rider to do what he physically cannot cope with. Don't put the rider in the position that creates the anxiety in the horse in the first place."

In setting up cavalletti, Page uses the measurements of six feet equaling one walking stride of the horse, and twelve feet one trotting stride. He uses eighteen feet as one trotting stride from a vertical to another fence, and twenty-four feet as one cantering stride between two obstacles. The eighteen foot measurement can be used to make a horse trot over a cross rail and then canter one stride to a vertical.

In his retraining of problem horses and his infrequent clinics, Page frequently finds himself curing horses who do not move forward to the second part of an in-and-out or combination obstacle. If you step back and analyze the problem, he feels, in

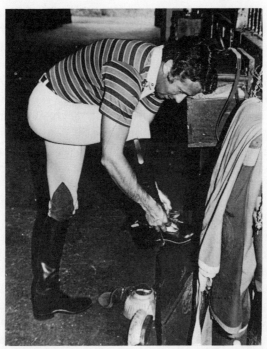

Michael Page preparing for a training session at The Hill in North Salem, New York. *Photo by Sue Maynard.*

most cases it is a "passive" rider who creates the hanging back problem in the first place because of the way he rides the horse on the approach to a fence.

"Once the rider's problems are dealt with," the veteran Olympian continues, "you begin to work with the horse. I feel if you keep the combination at one stride all you will do is ride stronger and crash and crash again into the 'out' portion. However, if you widen the in-and-out to two strides, you give the horse more time to work out the solution for himself. The rider encourages the horse to go forward as he lands over the 'in,' using his aids and a stick if necessary. The extra stride gives the horse the room to move forward. Many horses develop a tendency to hang back after jumping too high over the 'in.' The two-stride approach gives them the time to make the adjustment to going forward quickly to the 'out' or second part of the combination."

When it comes to refusals, Page blames them on the horse's loss of confidence in the rider. The rider must support the horse with his aids, get him to the proper point from which to leave the ground, and not interfere with the horse from that point onward.

An analysis of the two horses he rode in his Olympic and Pan American Games successes, and how Page worked with them, gives further insight into his deep, analytic approach to the horse-and-rider relationship. He recalled:

"Grasshopper was a true freak, only fifteen hands high, but a tremendous bundle of energy and a true event horse of world class. The problem was that he wasn't a mechanical animal, and he wasn't as good when he was not using his considerable abilities to the maximum. He was a superb three-day event horse, but not a very good horse in a one-day event. Many experts felt he should have been good, and under control, at one-day events or team trials. But he would just be getting warmed-up after going the five miles of those lesser events. If it was less than that distance, he would literally stop at a cross rail.

"Grasshopper, by a Thoroughbred stallion, Tudor, out of a Connemara pony mare, already was of world class when I got him. The problem was not to be 'Germanic' in my treatment of him, which frequently made both him and me a coach's nightmare. If the coach's schedule for the day was that all the horses would canter around a track at four hundred meters per minute, there was no way that Grasshopper would be one of the group.

"For all his energy and virtually tear-away character, he was not

Grasshopper, "a true freak" but a superb event horse at the international level, and Michael Page competing in the dressage phase of the Pebble Beach, California, Trials in 1961. This combination won individual Gold Medals in the 1959 and 1963 Pan American Games.

a brilliantly fast horse. If the other team horses breezed an eighth of a mile in twelve seconds, Grasshopper would go in :14, two seconds slower. But if you went around a racetrack twenty times the other horses would be slowed to a walk, and Grasshopper still would be going an eighth in :14."

Riding the pony-sized freak, Page won the Gold individual and team Silver Medals at the 1959 Pan American Games, finished seventeenth individually in the Rome Olympics in 1960, won the individual and team Gold in the 1963 Pan American Games in Brazil, and in 1964 at Tokyo finished fourth, missing an individual Bronze Medal by one-fifth of a point, and won a team Silver Medal.

"By this time I was spending virtually all my time riding," he explained. "I spent nearly the entire four years between Rome and Tokyo riding and competing in Europe. I felt it was time I went to work in our family's packaging business. But after two years I had the opportunity to get Foster and prepare for Mexico City, so I took it.

"Foster was also by Tudor, but out of a 7/8s Thoroughbred mare who had been a top international eventer. When he was young he had fallen at a ditch while hunting in Ireland, and nearly drowned. So he had an instinctive, psychological phobia about water, and when he had a stop at the water in the World Championships at Burghley, England, he almost had a 'break down' from the resulting 'schooling.'

"My wife, Georgette, was Foster's groom (and not yet my wife) and she understood him. He was a horse who could not be dominated, but had to be cajoled. He was the exact opposite of Grasshopper in many ways. You had to make Foster feel he was in control of the situation, running away with you. You never could take a good hold of him. With Grasshopper, on the other hand, you just took a double handful on the reins, hung on, and off you went.

"Foster's mind would work something like this: 'I really don't believe you want me to run this fast, so I'll go faster.' He had to be sort of 'snugged down' so he would think you wanted him to slow down, and then he would speed up. For six months Lars Sederholm and I worked to create in him an instinctive move forward in response to my legs, to condition his reflexes to 'forward' rather than looking around where he was going first. I entered him in events but didn't worry about dressage or show jumping. All I wanted to instill in him was the idea that he was 'running away' with me on the cross-country.

"Foster was not a brilliantly fast horse, but he had adequate speed, and was a very solid, fit horse, superb in being able to stay in top condition. At Mexico we had the second-fastest cross-country time, partially because we went before the rains flooded the course."

Riding Foster, Michael Page was third individually at the 1967 Pan American Games in Winnipeg, adding an individual Bronze to the team Gold Medal. A year later at Mexico Page and Foster won the Bronze Medal as individuals, while the USET took the team Silver. Then, Page decided, "I had been very fortunate to be so

Michael Page riding Foster in the cross-country at the 1968 Mexico Olympic Games, where they had the second-fastest time in that phase of the three-day event and won the Bronze Medal.

successful, but I just couldn't expect this success to continue with the time I had available. I now was married and twenty-nine years old and I really had to get serious about the business of earning a living.

"Luckily, my wife and I share the same interests. We keep our horses at The Hill, in North Salem, New York. I go to work and she rides and longes in the morning. I ride almost every night. I'm also quite busy judging. When I'm not, I'm able to show in the jumper division on weekends. I don't feel any pressure to be 'Number One' as I might be if I still were eventing. So now I get the pure pleasure out of riding, without any of the pressures.

"I was thinking seriously about trying out for the 1976 USET show jumping squad with Singapore, with whom I had been working for three years. But I had the opportunity to coach the

Pausing during a training session, Michael Page discusses his progress with his wife, Georgette. Mike is mounted on Newton's Law, while Georgette holds Highwater Mark. Both are sons of Blue Murmur. *Photo by Sue Maynard.*

Canadian three-day event team on a three-and-a-half day per week basis, so I took it and we let Kathy Kusner take over Singapore." Bernie Traurig bought the talented gray late in 1976.

Singapore was a Thoroughbred who had raced. Only eight years old when Page began working with him, "he had no basic trust in the people he had been associated with. My biggest problem was to get him to believe that what he was being asked to do wouldn't hurt him. It took two-and-a-half years for him to get to where he would use his natural instinct to move forward and forget the possibility of punishment if he failed.

"I was in the position to give Singapore the time he needed. He was ridden twice a day, every day. But since I am not a professional I could spend the time and get him to relax and let him do what he was capable of, without having to rush him to be a winner in the show ring. Singapore wasn't a refuser nor a rusher, he was just a very spooky horse. He was a natural jumper, but he distrusted the idea of people being around a fence. He is easier to ride in the show ring than the schooling area to this day.

"A spooky horse will whirl away and shy at something strange. But if the horse is schooled to respect the rider's aids and the rider can use them independently, then the horse may 'look' at the thing that might spook him but still react to the rider's legs and be obedient. Singapore also was a horse who didn't like going deep into the corners of the ring, but could jump a clear round because of his talent. A horse with lesser problems might have had less talent, so it might have been more difficult to get the same clear round with him. As a horseman, which horse do you go on with?"

Another reclamation project of Michael Page was Night Club, a "super-sensitive, unraced Thoroughbred who had completely rebelled against a rider-trainer who tried to dominate him. He became very rigid in his style of jumping, with his head drawn in. He wouldn't go forward into the rider's hands. It took months and months of work on the flat and over cavalletti."

Night Club went on to become a fine equitation mount, carrying Michael Hart into second place in the 1976 American

Singapore, a horse with no basic trust in people when Michael Page began working with him, stretching out for a spread fence at the Washington, D.C., Horse Show in 1975.

Horse Shows Association Medal finals, and in 1977 being the mount of Elizabeth Sheehan, who won the Medal finals. Adds Page: "Sometimes it all comes back to 'haunt' you and you think of how this talented horse could have been ruined. But there is no 'trick' to training, just figuring out what the horse needs and having the patience to give him what he needs, which may be the biggest 'trick' of all."

With his business and judging demands taking so much of his time, Page has time to give only one or two instructional clinics each year. "It's quite demanding to stage a good clinic," he admitted, "and it certainly takes more out of me, physically and mentally, than judging. Most professional horsemen don't like the idea of guest instructors. They fear that someone else could raise

Michael Page competing at the Farmington, Connecticut, Horse Show in 1975 aboard Night Club, another problem horse he retrained into a solid equitation mount.

Michael Page and Night Club showing fine hunter style at the Ox Ridge Hunt Club Horse Show in 1975. A year later Michael Hart finished second in the American Horse Shows Association finals on Night Club.

questions in the minds of their pupils, or the pupils' parents, about their own training techniques. Or they think that bringing in someone else lessens their own professional stature."

During the sessions of the clinic I saw and heard the following:

"I want you to feel that the back of the horse is the only place to be, the only place you feel comfortable. You're going to divide your body up into pieces, and then put them all together. Now everyone smile—for the last time—and take the rail at the sitting trot without stirrups."

"Don't look down at the ground, look up at the ceiling. Pull your legs down, touch the ground with them. Now the posting trot (without stirrups), without looking down, reins short enough to guide, hands out in front of you."

"The leg, to be used, has to be on the horse, not bobbing out and disturbing the air. Feel the horse all the way down your leg. Keep your leg on the horse, massaging him. Touch your right toe with your left hand without moving your legs. Lean back and put

Michael Page schooling Newton's Law over an oxer at The Hill. Note Page's concentration on the next fence. *Photo by Sue Maynard.*

your head on your horse's rump without moving the legs. This is harder when we'll do it over the top of a fence—but we have to start somewhere!"

"We want to strengthen our ability to communicate in a much shorter period of time. It can take three strides if you're weak in your aids, or one stride if you're strong."

One of the riders explained that she used a touch of her toe to cue her young horse to canter. Page replied, "That's fine, but what is your objective? Is it to have the best 'toe canter' horse in the World? This is not your ultimate aim. The 'toe canter' horse can't react coming into a fence unless he has been trained to respond to the proper aids."

"Sit and suffer at the canter on that frisky green horse. You have to give a little to get a little. You have to sacrifice some obedience to get that horse going forward. Going forward is more important than absolute obedience. It's all right if a horse plays a little when you start riding him."

The horse creating the most problems at one session was a green

"Good boy, you did fine," seems to be Michael Page's message to Newton's Law. Although horse and rider obviously have finished serious work, note the near perfect leg position of the rider. *Photo by Sue Maynard.*

hunter who had been recently purchased by a junior rider. The horse persisted in running out to the right on one line of the low schooling course. The rider was not using her crop and spur strongly enough on her mount's right side. "I want to see you draw some blood, I'm not kidding," Page urged. "He's got to respect your legs and move away from that right spur. He has to fear your leg more than he does that fence." Once the horse went over the fence the "guide" rail on the right side was removed and he then was ridden over the line four times. "Now walk and pat him," Page directed. "I don't see any marks on his sides. Did you call that kicking a horse—or exercising your knees?"

Page was overstating the situation, he explained later, but he emphasized: "The horse has to respect the rider's legs. He must be willing to go forward. That is basic to effective riding."

5 Ian Millar: The "Canadian-American" Training System

Ian Miller doesn't have dual citizenship, but the slender Canadian Olympic show jumping rider credits American horsemen for much of the improvement in his riding style, along with supplying him with most of the fine hunters and jumpers he is riding to victories in North American show rings.

But the thirty-year-old resident of Perth, Ontario (near Ottawa), also believes the "loose" Canadian Equestrian Team (CET) organization allowed him to move up rapidly to international competition, which he might not have been able to do had he lived "south" of the American-Canadian border.

And although Canadian nationalism is running high among his countrymen, ever alert to fight encroaching American influence, Millar considers the remarks of the CET show jumping coach at Montreal, American professional Carl Knee, that he was "more American in his outlook" toward riding, was "definitely a compliment."

"The 'American way' of riding and showing opens up a tremendous potential area of development as to what you can do with your body," the articulate horseman begins. "And because of the demand for athletic and speedy show jumping horses in international competition, that means you are generally using Thoroughbreds. They are a bit flighty so you must learn to sit still. It is especially important for a tall rider, like myself. Being six-feet, one-inch is an advantage because your long leg leads to a secure position in the saddle, and leads to better balance on turns and over an oxer. The disadvantage is that the long upper body

Ian Millar and Randy Roy taking notes on the course set up for the 1977 American Gold Cup in Philadelphia. *Photo by Sue Maynard.*

Canadian Ian Millar's 1976 Olympic mount, Count Down, carries him high and wide over a water jump at the Lake Placid Horse Show.

Brother Sam is one of Ian Millar's brightest hopes for the 1980 Olympic Games in Moscow. Here they leap an oxer on the 1977 American Gold Cup course designed by Robert Jolicoeur. They finished fifth. *Photo by Sue Maynard.*

must be in balance at all times, otherwise you can look very awkward. A small rider left behind, or a bit in advance of the horse, isn't very noticeable. A tall rider is."

When it comes to horseflesh, Millar also might be considered something of a traitor to Canada's long-established pattern of breeding hunters and jumpers who are half to three-quarters to 15/16ths Thoroughbred. He explains that such horses "were good show jumpers over vertical fences, when a horse was competing in small rings and had to have a good temperament. But the wide oxers, long distances between combinations and the big, outdoor Grand Prix courses have caught up with them. The Thoroughbreds, and the German Hanoverians, have tremendous natural impulsion that is common to all good international level jumpers. At that level, the horse has to do some of it on his own. So now you need a Thoroughbred (of the right temperament) even in the hunter ring. The half-bred or three-quarters bred may make a junior or amateur jumper, but you see very, very few of them on the Grand Prix circuit."

It was a three-quarter bred, however, that got Millar started on his serious riding career, he recalls. "I began taking lessons at fifteen. My parents would pay for one per week, and it was up to me to earn money for more lessons, which I did. Nancy Woods and I became partners. We'd buy horses, try them as jumpers, then sell them if they didn't work out. That's how we got War Machine, in trade for a junior horse. He was a big, 17-hand bully, a runaway rogue with ability. Running away was his evasion. If you let him run he'd soon give it up. Basically I just had to show him who was boss; I also took him hunting, which seems to work wonders with some horses."

Ottawa is 275 miles from Toronto, which is the hub of CET activity. So Ian and his new wife just loaded War Machine up each weekend, went to Toronto, did pretty well, and got invited to ride for the Canadian team—"It was just that simple. I wasn't quite ready that year—1969—but the next year I went to the Washington, D.C., Horse Show, got some ribbons and great experience, the type I couldn't afford to get paying out of my own pocket."

In 1971 Ian and War Machine finished fifth in the Pan American Games trials and were picked as spares. Doug Cudney bought War Machine and gave him to Millar to ride, and also gave him his veterans, Shoeman and Beefeater, as reserve horses. He went to Munich in 1972 as the spare, but . . . "Barbara Kerr's Magnor got hurt the day before the team event," he remembered with a grimace. "So at 6 P.M. I was told I'd ride the next day. Shoeman, a stable old pro, helped us finish sixth."

Millar felt his Olympic and Pan American exposure would attract Ottawa-area sponsors to back him with good horses, but nothing worked out until he met Carl and Jackie Morold, who had bought an old farm with a three-stall log barn. Late in 1973 they became his sponsors and built up what is now Dwyer Hill Farm, an enormous operation with over one hundred stalls, fifty boarders, a stallion, two indoor arenas, and a fine string of hunters and jumpers ridden by one of North America's best riders.

Jackie Morold, a childhood friend of former United States Equestrian Team rider George Morris, brought the top instructor to the new farm for some clinics, and he opened Millar's eyes to the range of equestrian refinement possible.

"I went to Florida with a couple of green horses in 1974 and

71

spent a month working with George before the circuit started," he said. "I just couldn't get enough of the work. American juniors get this education from the first time they put a leg over a horse. I had been an unconventional, seat-of-the-pants rider until then, never paying much attention to style and technique. Morris's clinics got me intrigued with systematic training, with the hunter ring as a basic approach to jumping. At the time I wasn't flowing with my hunters. It took a good year to get with my hunters, and I still spend a lot of time studying at the hunter ring."

Except for Virginia Clay, the overall open conformation hunter champion of the 1977 Florida circuit, all of Dwyer Hill's hunters are brought along with the idea that eventually they will become international jumpers. Virginia Clay, brought from Mrs. Swanee Cunningham in Virginia as a green-broke three-year-old, hasn't the desire to be a jumper, and is too nice a hunter to change, says Millar. Cease Fire, a green conformation hunter, was bought from Jim Kohn while Another Brother, first-year green working in 1977, was purchased from Joe Darby.

Except for Count Down, bred by E.P. Taylor in Canada, Millar's

Ian Millar and Springer competing in the American Gold Cup in Philadelphia's Veterans Stadium in 1977. *Photo by Sue Maynard.*

Ian Millar is a study in concentration as he prepares to compete in a Canadian Grand Prix on Hawk. *Courtesy Peachey Picture.*

other jumpers came from the United States. Count Down broke down at the track as a three-year-old but was "strong and difficult" as a hunter. However, Millar worked hard with him, won one Grand Prix and was second in another, and jumped six feet, nine inches on him at the Royal Winter Fair in Toronto.

Brother Sam, another seventeen-hand Thoroughbred, started out as a conformation hunter and in Florida in 1976 went open

73

Ian Millar and his temperamental mare, Springer, tied for first in the puissance class in the 1976 National Horse Show in Madison Square Garden. Could anyone ask for a horse to make more of an effort? *Photo by Sue Maynard.*

conformation and intermediate jumper, an unusual combination. Hawk, also purchased from Jim Kohn, was "just awful" when he began jumping in 1976.

"If he couldn't run away, he wouldn't go at all," Millar admitted. "But he was only five years old. At the end of Florida we'd come to an understanding and he's been a winner ever since. He won three modified Grand Prix classes in Canada in 1976, but had some difficulties in intermediate classes. He's extremely talented with great impulsion and a tremendous desire to jump clean.

"Springer, a 16.1 mare I got from Bernie Traurig, is a full sister to the good hunter Springdale. She is small but rides 'big,' a powerful mover with tremendous scope. However, she's 'all woman' and the most difficult horse I've ever had to ride. It has taken a long time to get with her, but during the 1976 Olympic trials she was third overall, with Count Down fourth and Brother Sam fifth. But her past inconsistency caused us to leave her out of the games. She was fourth in the Philadelphia Gold Cup afterwards, the first of four horses to have three clean rounds. She tied with Barney Ward and Wow at six feet nine inches in the puissance in Madison Square Garden. The only time she felt 'small' was when the wall went to seven feet. She's as nice a horse as I've ridden—when she'll allow herself to be ridden."

For the Moscow Olympics, Millar feels he has good depth in his string. Brother Sam could be the best by 1980 from a consistency and reliability standpoint. Millar feels he must learn the "little tricks:" shortening strides, maneuvering hard turns with tough distances, twisting to miss a rail. Right now he wants to jump in perfect hunter form, and not be a "slippery" jumper. Springer could be used in the individual event, with her disposition capable of producing the "impossible effort" if she totally commits herself to cooperating. Hawk could fit in, too, and Count Down, now eleven years old, would be much better than an empty stall to fall back on.

Millar describes Count Down as a "good" Olympic Games horse, but not a "great" one and says that "developing horses is the challenge. Count Down is now at the top level so it's not as intriguing to keep him there as it is to improve the others."

Millar believes that because he and trainer Randy Roy got involved rather late in their riding careers, "We may be hungrier for success, and spend more time observing, learning, and trying to move forward." From his observations Millar has concluded, "A horse seems to take on a certain identity after being ridden and trained by a certain horseman, the way the paintings of an artist have certain identifiable characteristics.

"I am especially impressed by certain riders' strong points. Dennis Murphy, I feel, has his horses shorten and lengthen strides beautifully, better than anyone else. I might not do it the same way, but I'm trying to gain the same objective. Bernie Traurig's horses are always so beautifully disciplined on the course, you never feel it's 'hit and miss' with him. Rodney Jenkins's horses are so round and soft, so elastic in the air, while Katie Monahan's horses are right up in front of her, ready and balanced.

"If one rider could combine all those strong points, learn to do all those things. . . . The difference now between first place and tenth can be a fraction of a second. There are so many good riders and good horses that you win classes by a 'nose,' not by 'ten lengths.' That's why I feel you have to travel, to see all the great riders. I've absorbed all I can from the other Canadians."

Among those international riders Millar would like to spend more time studying are David Broome, for his controlled, disciplined approach; Eddie Macken, for the use of the hackamore, and the way his horses trust him; and Kevin Bacon, for his balance, control, and competitive drive.

When it comes to training philosophy, Millar believes that it takes "discipline with relaxation" to win hunter classes and "getting a Thoroughbred quiet is quite a feat. You can't force it or you'll get the tense, rigid type of obedience that is obvious. Yet you can't adopt the older European idea of taking three or more years to get a horse ready to show. The economics of the business almost force the approach of 'off the track today, in the schooling show tomorrow,' he observes, noting:

"A horse like Kevin Bacon's Chichester would have been discarded in North America as not having enough scope. Or else he would have moved up the scale of classes too fast and would have lost his confidence. But he's jumping fences he shouldn't be capable of jumping because of his heart and his confidence in Kevin. He's been given time to learn to wiggle and wriggle through the fences. Some horses may be five-cents short on ability, but if you give them time. . . ."

Millar bases his training on a disciplined system of longeing through a series of voice commands, and points out that he often rides four horses in a Grand Prix class and simply wouldn't have enough time to ride them all prior to a class or school them extensively before going into the ring. But using the method of voice commands on the longe line, Millar says, his girl grooms can tell him how the horses are behaving and he can adjust his handling of them accordingly. At a show footing can be slippery or deep, he points out, and the horse has to be controllable at the end of the longe line. The Canadian winters also make turning out impossible, and the longeing system enables Dwyer Hill Farm to keep horses' temperaments down to "a dull roar."

"It's my safety factor," Millar declares. "If they get too strong they can injure themselves; but some trainers knock the system

Ian Millar competing in a hunter class on Virginia Clay, a top winner both in conformation and in working hunter classes.

Ian Millar and Brother Sam race through the finish flags at the 1977 American Gold Cup. The horse, who was just one year out of hunter classes, finished fifth. *Photo by Sue Maynard.*

because it's unconventional." Millar tacks up his young horses with a bridle and a soft bit, side reins, a standing martingale, and saddle. He hooks the longe line on one bit ring, passes it over the horse's poll and then through the near side bit ring. Naturally, he uses a longe whip, mainly pointing at the horse's hind quarters.

"A young Thoroughbred doesn't want a lot of hard riding, especially from a rider of my weight," he notes. "If you're starting them out in good weather, you turn them out before longeing. I use the word *stay* instead of *whoa* when I want a horse to stop from the walk, and stay in place. I use *whoa* when I want a horse to go from the 'trot-on' to the walk. When I say *trot-on* my voice goes up on the *on*. By using different inflections—*caanter* for a slow canter, *can-turr* for a faster one—you can carry on a real conversation with them.

"Of course, you've got to use good sense. When they're fresh you don't ask them to 'stay' right away. Tell them to 'trot-on' because they'll do it anyway, but if you use your voice command they'll think it's your idea. You wait until they start to slow down and give in before you ask them to decrease speed. Let them go to 'stay' in four or five steps. By using good sense you get them to saying 'yes.' The basic salesman's tool is to get them thinking positively, right? We want them submissive, but not resentful. You use gentle tugs, but when you do generally they will get to tossing their heads, and that's why you need the martingale. They will hit their noses on it and drop their heads and 'stay.' Gradually you 'wean' them from your voice to your aids when you do more riding. The use of the longe line and voice commands avoids the need to use tranquilizers."

Millar, like most horsemen, believes in designing a system of gymnastics—jumps in a line—to shore up a weakness that a horse has. He leads into them with cavalletti, with the poles either on the ground or raised a few inches. If they're off the ground, the horse has to use his knees more—appropriate for a jumper, but not for a hunter.

"Brother Sam," he explains, "has a long, open stride and sometimes moves too close to the ground and doesn't use his shoulders. With him I'll set three poles three feet apart, raised four inches off the ground (to the top of the poles is about seven inches). I leave six feet between the last pole and a low vertical, and then there's eighteen feet to a second vertical, with a ground line rolled well out. Trotting over the cavalletti makes him shorten stride and use his shoulders. He has to use his shoulders to jump the first fence, then shorten again to avoid the ground line and jump the second.

"Another horse might jump oxers well but get 'rammy' at verticals. You set up a gymnastic exercise to cure that, and before long he's doing the verticals great and landing in the middle of oxers, so you have to go backwards and hit a balance. That's the secret. But of course when you're schooling with a certain show in mind you have to remember that certain shows have certain features on their courses and that certain course-builders emphasize certain things."

Millar also believes it is important to have a good "ground man," like Dwyer Hill trainer Randy Roy, explaining: "A good hunter-jumper trainer is a long-range thinker. A competitive rider may be just thinking of the one class, and in the heat of battle you're not always tempered with prudence. The ups and downs of each class do not affect Randy, who is more concerned with the long range ups and downs. This is a good checks and balances system that we have worked out, although it took a while for me to learn how to yield."

The Canadian rider believes the most common problem with young horses is that they get a little quick and won't shorten strides as a result. "With this type of horse you can't usually ease off his mouth on the approach or he winds up with an inverted spine and neck, as opposed to rounding his back and dropping his head and neck," he explains. "I'd use the same type of gymnastic as before, trotting poles three feet apart, then six feet to a little vertical, then eighteen feet to another. Once he's softening up for the stride in between the two verticals you might make the second into a low oxer and gradually spread it to the point where he has to round himself in the air."

Another common problem is a horse that relies on being tight and fast with his knees instead of shortening stride on the approach to a jump. "The rider's eye recognizes he and his horse will be deep to a fence," Millar points out, "so the last few strides he closes his legs and tries to knock six to eight inches off each stride. But the horse won't shorten and gets deep, yet avoids trouble by being quick with his legs. This isn't good in a hunter class and will catch up with him in the jumper ring, as the fences get bigger. In addition, the deep spots interfere with their forward flow into a combination or the next jump."

Here again Millar uses his same gymnastics setup: the three trotting poles three feet apart, then six to nine feet to a small vertical, then eighteen feet to another vertical, and then twenty feet to a third. The ground rail for the second fence would be advanced quite a bit, cutting the eighteen feet distance to about twelve feet. This would force the horse to shorten stride for the second fence, and then canter off to another fence.

"When the horse shortens up he has all kinds of room to fold up his front legs," Millar emphasizes. "With the third fence twenty feet away it comes close to 'loose schooling' once he comes over the first trot pole. You release him and let him work out the problems himself. If he gets strong he'll bang over the poles. If he gets to dropping behind it'll be the same thing. He's forced to learn to go at the right pace and learn that it's not the rider who's his enemy, it's the fence. So the problem to be solved is the fence, and the rider is there to help him solve the problem. If you can get the horse thinking that way, he'll learn to appreciate being rated, lengthened or shortened, between jumps.

"Many horses get tense and quick through lack of confidence, and solve their problems by going faster. Repetition through gymnastics will teach one to gain confidence in his own ability. It's a false confidence in a way. He'll be able to jump well because it's pre-established for him. But you still have to put a jump in the middle of the ring eventually and canter them over it: they have to learn to put all their training into practice. And a rider with an inconsistent eye will need all the confidence he's attained over the gymnastics, too."

If a horse drifts to the left, Millar would lay a rail on the ground on that side of the fence. As the horse trots to the takeoff point he will wind up stepping on the pole unless he meets the fence squarely in the center. Crossed poles in the shape of an "X" will cure a horse who twists behind. A rail from the ground to the jump will also cure this problem.

Millar warns, however, that "too much pressure on the horse's jumping form, making gymnastics too difficult for his abilities, will make him evade shortening his stride by drifting to gain the extra foot on a stride, or twisting behind. Gymnastics is a powerful tool, but it must be used with discretion or it can create as many problems as it solves.

"Hunters, big scopey horses, many times jump with their bodies and not with their legs. Gymnastics and tight distances force them

The unusual headgear Ian Millar is wearing contains a camera, which records his round aboard Springer for showing over Canadian television.

Ian Millar and Springer competing in a Canadian Grand Prix event. *Courtesy Peachey Picture.*

to be correct with their legs. If necessary you build the jump up under them to where it's bigger than they can handle with their bodies. Usually a hunter fence does not make a hunter reach his limit of ability. Then he figures 'it's not as easy to jump big any more, I'll be tidier and use my leg.' But more size in the jump is absolutely your last resort, because you are chancing a hard rap or even a fall and then a lack of confidence.

"Some trainers believe repetition through gymnastics or over fences will get a horse that jumps with his body tired, and then he'll jump lower, hit it, and hopefully get tighter with his legs. I'd rather not jump them too much.

"But if everything goes fine in schooling, then I've wasted my time—all I've done is conditioned the horse. You do work toward exposing weaknesses. If a confident, experienced horse bangs a fence, it doesn't bother me. But self-confidence is so important to a young horse. If one of those clobbers a fence I'm worried.

"I'll pull up and make sure he's not hurt, then confer with Randy. We'll lower the fence, change the ground line, or do

Young Jonathon Millar gets a ride on Brother Sam from his father, Ian Millar, and Dwyer Hill Farm trainer Randy Roy, left, at a show at SamSon Farm in Canada.

Ian Millar saluting the judges prior to competing in a jumper class on Hawk, one of his hopefuls for the 1980 Olympic Games in Moscow. *Courtesy Peachey Picture.*

whatever is necessary to get him over it in a confident manner.

"If there's a wreck in the ring and it's a rider's error the only emotion stirred in me is regret, self-blame. If it's not my fault then I'm angry—but it'll prove nothing to allow it to show. I finish the round as best I can, get off, think it through, and then talk to Randy. In retrospect, there may have been something I could have done better. Anger shown by a rider on a horse is quickly noticed by others; I try very hard to avoid it.

"I've been very lucky that I haven't had to worry too much about refusals or run outs. I've been lucky never to have had many stoppers. As a rule most of my horses will jump into a fence from an impossible spot—they seem to feel they should go forward. So if one of them does refuse there's usually a good reason for it. It might be a physical reason, or the distance or footing. Maybe he's not comfortable in his back or shoulders.

"With the tough fences we have now, a horse has to want to work with you and for you. You can't bully him. That's why I find training is a two-man job, like sharpening a knife to a very fine edge. It requires a lot of observation. Competition at big shows is so specialized that the little form problems can make the difference between first and fifth.

"With such keen competition winning, even with a good horse cutting corners and at speed, means the winner stayed within the limit of what is possible. The fastest four-fault round went beyond what was possible. There is no shortage of good horses and good riders. It's almost to the point that to win you have to be lucky—and someone else has to be unlucky."

6 John Mullins:
The Mouth Can Unlock the Brain

A good horse has to be a smart horse, especially when it comes to showing him in more than one type of competition. For intelligence, a horse obviously has to have a brain. And John Mullins, one of the top trainers of Appaloosas in the East, believes the key to unlocking a horse's brain lies in his mouth.

"When I was showing Little Navajo Joe in the early 1960s," Mullins explained, "people would see us win a race or a timed event, then come into the ring and win a pleasure class and many of them would tell each other 'He's using drugs. The horse is a running fool in a race. He can't calm down for a pleasure class without drugs.'

"But, of course, they were wrong. I've never used a tranquilizer on a horse as long as I've been training—even for dealing with a sick or unruly horse, or in transporting one, I feel there's got to be another way than using a tranquilizer. The secret was in training Joe properly, and in using a different bit for every type of event.

"Joe was 'a running fool' in a race; most horses do get excited when they're raced or worked on a racetrack. But he was trained to be a gentleman at shows, and at home, and he performed to that training. It's training, knowing the horse's breeding, and using a different bit for a different event that will make a truly versatile horse."

Mullins showed Joe in a sweetwater bit, without too long a shank, in pleasure classes. When he was a "junior horse" he was shown in a bosal. In games or timed events he wore a mechanical hackamore with a braided noseband and a curb chain. Little

John Mullins and Little Navajo Joe accepting a Greater Eastern Appaloosa Region (GEAR) award.

Navajo Joe didn't need a tie-down or martingale for timed events, or roping, although most horses will. In English pleasure Mullins used a rubber or leather-covered "D" snaffle. For racing, he used a racing "D" snaffle, which is a little thinner. He still uses these bits on Joe's sons and daughters, and they, too, respond to the change in equipment with a change in behavior.

"When you're at a show, have finished a timed event and are preparing for a pleasure class," he advises, "the horse can sense the change by the way you ride him. In a race you're riding with short stirrups and sitting forward on him; you're doing the same, but to a lesser extent, in a games class. But if you drop your stirrups, sit deep, change your equipment, and then ride him softly and quietly, he should respond and quiet down for you.

"There are a lot of people who believe in working a horse down for a pleasure class by busting him out in a long gallop, to get rid of his excess energy in one burst. I think this only succeeds in getting him 'hot' and keeping him 'hot'—but there is the occasional horse that does settle right down after a good run. You can't make a rule that will apply to every horse."

Mullins, who also has trained Quarter Horses, Arabs, Paints, Thoroughbreds, and grade horses, believes most Appaloosa breeders and shows have stressed versatility more than other Western breeds and breed shows. An Appaloosa-owner since the late 1950s, when his first horses were in the first one thousand registered, he traces the increased versatility of the breed to the infusion of more "hot" blood, mainly through the Thoroughbred.

"There are undesirable horses in any breed," he admits. "I've had Appys who wouldn't work, and there are 'fired-up' Quarter Horses and Appys just as there are 'fired up' Thoroughbreds. This comes from too much concentration of certain bloodlines in the horse. That's why Three Bars was such a good influence on Quarter Horses: he had the Thoroughbred speed but he was very quiet. His offspring made good pleasure horses.

"The hot blood enables a horse to learn quicker, as well as contributing to a more streamlined appearance. When the Appaloosa registry started, we had to do something. Too much of the Nez Perce stock had been allowed to become inbred or range bred with draft stock. This influence especially was noticed in the long, ugly heads of many early Appys. Showing dictated the development of a better-looking horse, and racing brought in the Thoroughbred for more speed.

"Appaloosa breeders do not want to compete with either the Quarter Horse or the Thoroughbred in racing. We program races that are a little longer than the four-hundred-forty- to five-hundred-yard Quarter Horse races; most of ours are a half-mile or five-eighths of a mile, and around one turn. This is why we go to the Thoroughbred, rather than the Quarter Horse, for speed. Our distances dictate a little more size and good muscling to get out of the gate fast."

Mullins, a native of Plainview, Nebraska, grew up on a farm that was only a few miles from ranching territory. His father taught him to ride bareback—"the best way to learn balance, and you can't ride well without that." After graduating from high school he went to work for a friend of his father's, Howard Pitzer, a ranch operator and horse breeder in Ericson, Nebraska.

John recalls his first exposure to the Appaloosa when Pitzer bought twenty Appy mares, bred them to his Quarter Horse stallions, then sold them all when the first ten foals were solid-colored. But Mullins purchased Navajo Turquoise of AA, who had placed in a national show as a yearling, the following year and she's been the "blue hen" of his breeding program—after an early disaster.

"I had her entered in nine events as a two-year-old at the 1960 National at Sioux City, Iowa," he remembered. "I took her to my father's farm the day before the show, rode her, and turned her out in a pasture. She became attracted to a horse in a nearby pasture, ran into the fence, and gashed herself all the way down her right hind leg and into the hoof. It left her with almost a club foot. So I bred her to a good ranch using Quarter Horse of Mr. Pitzer's, Little Fob, and bred her back the following year." The foals were Little Navajo Joe and Little Navajo Wrangler, now a top roping gelding owned by Joel Cohen of Pittsford, New York.

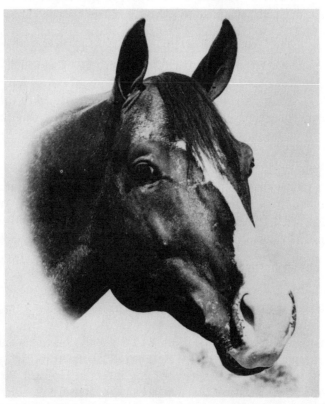

Little Navajo Joe, an unusually versatile Appaloosa, shows the muscular jaws of his Quarter Horse sire, Little Fob, and the distinctive blaze he passes on to most of his Appaloosa foals.

Turquoise was left in Nebraska when Mullins moved to New York state to train for an Appaloosa breeder. He left a few months later to purchase his own eighty-acre farm in Elba, New York, about midway between Buffalo and Rochester. Little Navajo Joe came East, with his dam and a Quarter broodmare, and soon went into training.

The black stallion with the white blanket, blaze, and three white socks soon began making a name for himself with wins in halter, pleasure, reining, Western riding, stump and barrel racing, roping, and racing. He has passed on this versatility to his offspring. Two (Little Mona Jo and Little Navajo Britches) have placed in National shows in reining, and Joe also has won Greater Eastern Appaloosa Region (GEAR) awards for get of sire despite never having been bred to a national champion mare. He's accomplished this with a limited advertising budget, too.

But as grand a horse as Little Navajo Joe is, Mullins admits he not only passes on his blaze and white socks to his offspring—one mark of his prepotency—but also outproduces himself: his sons and daughters are better horses han he was. In the matter of color, so essential in an Appaloosa breeding program, Joe has produced a produced a steady eighty percent registered foals. The national average is about fifty percent registered offspring by Appaloosa stallions.

Mullins believes Little Navajo Joe's offspring have proved themselves in one of the most competitive areas of Appaloosa showing, noting that horses from the GEAR area have done well in National Appaloosa shows and that entries of thirty to forty horses are commonplace in pleasure classes in most GEAR shows.

"When I began training Joe I didn't have that many horses on the farm," Mullins recalls. "And I was able to work with him twice a day. This is the ideal way to train a young horse."

As a breeder, Mullins believes in private sales and usually sells his stock with four to six weeks of training, at two or three years of age. The new owner generally takes riding lessons on his new horse for a week or two under Mullins's supervision. "I learned early that you can't keep every colt you like," he asserted. "When a customer wants one and can pay what the horse is worth you have to let him go—even when you know the horse won't go as far in the show ring for that rider as he would with you showing him. Of course if the horse definitely is too spirited for that particular adult or youth rider, forget the sale. Don't misrepresent your horses."

Mullins finds his outside training usually is heaviest in March and April; owners want to begin showing in June. This means he must begin training his own stock in December and January and makes an indoor arena a necessity. As "cures" for working alone at the farm and getting on one "young, dumb" colt after another, Mullins talks to his horses frequently ("You have to talk to someone, or you'll turn into a mute," he jokes) and every so often he rides one of his older horses just to end the monotony of teaching the "A-B-C s" over and over.

In addition to breeding, showing, and training, Mullins also gives riding lessons: "You see so many mistakes made you are reminded to avoid them yourself. It's a good change of pace, you're performing a needed service for horse-lovers who have no other way to ride, and you never know when a student will advance to owning and showing."

Mullins uses his broodmares for lesson riders, and to avoid the monotony of going 'round and 'round the indoor arena tries to get his students outside on a trail ride at least once a month (if they ride once a week). This is good for both horses and riders.

As a breeder, he definitely does not believe in putting young stock out in a back pasture and forgetting about them. Young stock must be where you can look them over daily, and handle them often. They should have their feet trimmed at six months of age and those which need corrective shoeing should be shod with light plates.

"I'd rather not show weanlings," he states, "especially before they are weaned. The injury factor is too high. You have to take both the mare and foal in the trailer. You can't tie up the foal, and the mare may be hard to handle. The foal won't pay much attention to you in the ring with his dam whinnying from outside the ring or from the trailer. Then, too, you'll do best with a foal born in January or February, and I believe it's best to have your foals born when the grass is green. In New York state, this means April. I think a foal born later always will have a nicer coat and will be healthier, too.

"But, too, a halter futurity is a good advertisement for your stallion, so you nominate your best mare, based on her past record. You want good size, with a filled out, well-muscled frame. That's hard to have if they've just been weaned.

"I don't believe in longeing weanlings. It is too easy for them to get splints or puffs from a sudden stop. I like to lead my young

90

John Mullins races Little Navajo Joe around a barrel, one of several events the versatile Appaloosa competed in successfully.

stock from the back of a good, reliable horse. You jog and slow gallop to develop the longer stride that will catch a judge's eye. Too much longeing inside an arena shortens the stride—no matter what the age of the horse.

"I think automatic walkers are excellent to halter-break a youngster and excellent for exercising them. The walker should not be too small, and it should be enclosed by a fence so the horses can't wheel out. It should be a walker that can be reversed so the colts can be walked in either direction, and one that can be adjusted for both a slow and a fast walk is good. I'd never set one to the speed where it would make the colts trot, either. And you don't just hitch them to it and go away. You've got to keep an eye on them. No walker is fool-proof.

"A weanling should be taught to stand squarely—getting them to stand still is the main problem. You teach them to plant the right hind foot and then walk a half-step forward to square themselves up. The half-step isn't natural. Work at it for ten to fifteen minutes once a day; twice a day is better." When not being worked in hand, a weanling should be turned out with a few others so he gets used to being with other horses.

Mullins follows the same general training plan with a yearling— with one exception. He keeps them out of the bright sunlight

91

except for ten to fifteen minutes in a paddock daily. "The sun will ruin a coat, make a black horse become brown," he asserts. "Turn them out at night and bring them in during the day. You even keep a light sheet on them at shows."

Now, too, is the time to begin to pay attention to conformation, using sweat hoods to thin a colt's throat latch or neck. Mullins likes one that is plastic or smooth lined. If you're going to show the yearling in winter and spring shows, you'll have to blanket him and use the neck hood to train his mane. Don't be afraid to use two or even three blankets, and use a turn-out blanket when the colt gets outside. "The cold and wind will turn his hair right up," he warns. He likes blankets that are a one-piece design, closed in front, which are slipped over the colt's head. It's just two fewer straps that can be pulled out. Small tears should be sewn up before they become bigger. It's better to use blankets than to have a heated barn, Mullins feels.

Unless the yearling is unusually mature, or a race prospect, Mullins will not put a saddle on him until after Christmas. And the saddle is always preceded by two to four weeks of ground driving.

"I'll start driving them in November or so, after the show season is over," he explains. "I use a bosal, and later may move up to a bosal with a bar bit—don't be in a hurry to get the colt into a bit. I put the saddle on them, tie the stirrups under the belly, and put the driving lines through the stirrups.

"Never start ground-driving without a helper. Horses are used to being led, not walking ahead of you. Have someone lead the colt out, with you behind. That way they don't turn around and get themselves tangled up. Use your voice as well as your hands. When they are controllable from the ground, then they can be tried under saddle."

Mullins is light, and uses a light saddle on his yearlings. He'll generally longe them, with the saddle on, before riding, but again keeps it to a minimum. If the colt has an extremely cold back, he warms up the saddle pad before saddling him up. "Longe in as large a circle as you can, at least thirty feet," he advises. "If you work them on too small a cricle they get used to moving with their bodies curved and either carry their heads too far to the inside, or pull and carry it too far to the outside.

"When I get on, I start out with a walk or slow trot for about ten minutes. Fast galloping, backing, and hard stopping are the things you want to avoid. Then I'll go to a trot and slow gallop for ten to fifteen minutes, and walk the rest of the time—which shouldn't exceed thirty to forty-five minutes. An hour's riding—unless it's thirty minutes in the morning and the same in the afternoon or evening—is too much for a colt. With the time you spend cleaning him, tacking him, longeing him, riding him, and cooling him out you're spending well over an hour with him. I like to finish up quietly, with a stop and a back. I always back my horses after stopping them; it gets them in the habit of stopping in better balance. And after backing I want them to stop and stand. I want them thinking 'back' when they stop so they aren't spraddled out and out of balance. Later, when you're going into pivots and roll-backs, it is easier if the horse stops in a balanced position."

Mullins believes in trotting the colt into a canter or slow gallop. "Canter to me means 'canted,' slanted in body position to make it easier to go into the canter," he contends. "I use outside rein pressure on his neck, outside leg pressure, and a slight upward and forward shift of my body. The object is never to let the colt get on a wrong lead. Make sure he's right every time."

Mullins will not put a horse into a canter from a walk until he's been under saddle at least six months and thus is three years old. A couple more months and he may begin working at cantering from a standstill, which is a lot harder. (Many Western judges ask for it in ride-offs.) The important thing at this point is to go slowly and quietly and ride in large circles at the canter, tightening them up only if the colt insists on cantering too strongly. At the trot the colt can handle smaller circles, figure eight's, sweeping serpentines, and other basic ground movements.

"You have to remember that tighter circles tire the colt faster," he warns. "When the colt will work close to the walls of the indoor ring, it indicates he's ready to go into an outdoor ring and even into the fields—if the weather cooperates. If they're occasionally bulling into the middle of the ring, you have to stay in the ring. After a total of six weeks, it's time to stop. Turn him out at night, get him into your outdoor ring for ten to fifteen minutes of sunlight, and let him mature.

"If you're planning on showing him at all, you should only go to one or two shows just for the experience. It could be a small, local 'fun' show. Put the colt into a pleasure class. Don't do anything different that week, just ride him the day before the show. At the show you might have to ride him until he sweats (on

Some Appaloosa horse shows' trail horse classes require entries to prove how well they are ground-tied, as Little Navajo Joe is doing here.

a hot day), then wipe him off, and then go into the ring."

In pleasure classes, Western judges expect a horse at the lope, when asked to "stop," to break gait, trot one or two steps, walk one step and then stop and stand still. This is the type of "stop" a two- or three-year-old should be trained to do. An older pleasure horse should go from the lope to a stop with no extra steps.

With a three-year-old, Mullins is ready to begin flying lead changes after four to six weeks of training (in addition to the time spent under saddle at two), move on to harder stops, and begin roll-backs if the colt is entered in a reining futurity, as many of his colts are. The roll-back, he contends, is three procedures to be blended into one motion: stop, change leads, and come back. He teaches it by using the walls of his arena and the corner of his ring. Ride the colt past the corner, stop (briefly), turn into the corner, then come back out in the other direction.

The quarter-turn is helped by teaching the colt from the first to stop and then back. He already has his feet underneath him when he stops. The problem in the quarter-turn is to teach the colt to cross his front feet, not to rear up on his hind legs and jump over. The colt should be moved with the outside rein across the neck and the outside leg a bit behind the girth (the legs are on the girth for signals for changes of gait). The inside foot is a little ahead of the girth to point into the turn and shift the rider's weight slightly. The colt may need a little prompting with a crop or bat applied on the neck alongside the rein.

"If your colt is a quick-moving one, use protective bandages and boots," Mullins advises. "When it comes to backing, he should be able to go back longer distances. Don't let him stop when he wants to. Vary your pattern. I may go halfway across the arena one time, three to four steps another. Some judges ask you to back the full ten feet.

"For sliding stops you've got to be sure of your footing. Grass is often slick and dangerous. Dirt can be too sticky or too deep, such as straight sand. If you're going to show your colt in pleasure classes, he should be getting more work out in a pasture than he would in a ring. A horse worked by the rail gets too sour, and the expression of his ears often is noticed by the judge. The main thing to guard against is the colt speeding up and going too fast for a good pleasure gait.

"Working outside also helps you prepare your horse for trail classes. He should learn to go over natural obstacles such as rocks and logs, even if you have to lead him the first time. He has to learn to go into water and mud; then he won't get 'shook' if he's in a ring where the footing is somewhat loose. Working over natural obstacles keeps the horse alert and interested in what he's doing. There's nothing worse than a mechanical-moving and acting trail horse.

"When you have a reining futurity prospect, even showing him three or four times in reining will teach him the pattern. Shows and judges are starting to use different patterns, and that helps your training. You can't let the horse get ahead of you and anticipating where he's going to stop or turn. If you showed a pattern that had you run from right to left and then stop, at home you'd go in the other direction to practice. Never, never run the complete pattern. Do parts of it, but in different places from where they occur in the pattern.

"If you have a reining prospect, you should only show him in reining, pleasure, or Western riding classes. A three-year-old should not go to more than three or four shows and compete in reining if he's a futurity prospect. You could go to more shows and compete in pleasure or Western riding, however.

"I like futurities. It costs you a little more in entry fees but you have more entries, they are evenly matched because they all are the same age, there is more interest from owners and trainers, and you have a better chance for a larger payoff.

"In Appaloosa shows, Western pleasure seems to draw more entries than English pleasure, and I usually show in Western pleasure. I think a horse's conformation and size determines in

95

which events you should show him. Most Appaloosa judges seem to like good, easy gaits in both pleasure classes. Much depends on the show schedule. You couldn't work a horse down to where he'd look good in a Western pleasure class and then go into an English pleasure class and expect him to have enough animation to win. But changing bits could give him the idea that he should walk a little faster and move out a little more at the trot."

When a horse becomes four years old, Mullins would start him in timed events if the horse had the speed for them. From training for reining classes the colt has learned how to change leads, which he will utilize in stump or stake or barrel racing. Competing in games definitely "speeds up" a horse for pleasure classes, although a few will not be affected. Again, a change in equipment will help the horse realize he's to slow down and relax after competing in a timed event. In obstacle racing, Mullins stresses working at the trot and keeping the horse as close to the obstacle as possible. It's the closeness in the turns, not speed, that wins these events.

"If you need to use a noseband to keep your horse's mouth shut, put it on and keep it snug," he noted. "Even if the equipment is not permitted in the class, there's no rule that says you can't ride right up to the ring entrance before taking it off."

At the show, in addition to keeping a light sheet on your horse when he's not being ridden, Mullins advises tying him to the trailer by a strong rope attached to a well-fitting, strong halter. Avoid being careless around your own horse and other horses—some have been known to kick!

"When I see horses tied by their bridle reins at a show I'm of two minds," Mullins says. "I'd like to see those reins broken off by the horse to teach his owner a lesson; but I don't want to see the poor horse take the jab in the mouth from the bit before the reins give way. You spend all your time training and riding a horse so he'll have a soft mouth—then throw it all away by one careless act.

"Come to the show on time and put your time to good use. If you've shown before the judge previously and you have two horses at the show, you ought to know what type of horse he likes and know which of your horses to show in more classes than the other.

"Many people do not really know the rules for a class or the proper class procedure. You can learn by observation. I'll watch the ladies Western pleasure, for example. Does the judge ask for a walk, then a jog, then a lope? Or does he call for a jog, then a

John and Cleo Mullins with a few of the trophies won by their versatile black and white stallion Little Navajo Joe.

walk, and then a lope? Then you're ready when your turn comes.

"In a big pleasure class you can't afford to be overlooked by having too drab a saddle or clothing. You don't have to have a $500 turquoise necklace or a silver halter, but your clothing and tack should be neat, fit you well, and be presentable.

"First impressions are so important. Obviously you and your horse must be groomed to perfection. But your attitude must be 'up,' too. I tell my young students to move their horses along so they look alert, with their ears up. I tell them to 'Feel like you already have won the class when you go in the ring.' Don't go in with a 'born loser' expression.

"A child who shows horses, or competes in any sport, must learn how to lose as well as win—but you don't want him to be losing continuously and getting a defeatist attitude. A neighbor's son has undergone an almost unbelievable change in personality once his parents bought him a good horse (one of Little Navajo Joe's colts, I'm proud to say) he could win on. I always say it COSTS to keep a poor horse, it PAYS to keep a good one.

"Although a pleasure class is large, put your horse where he works the best. If I have a good 'rail horse,' that's where I ride him. I figure the judge will find me there. If he doesn't like the rail, come in a little. But don't be so obvious you're riding circles around the judge. If I were the judge I'd mark such a rider down.

"Listen to and watch the judge and ringmaster. In a Western show they will point to you and beckon you into the center of the ring. If you're not watching them they aren't going to give you ten chances. You'd be surprised how often you can miss a ribbon that way.

"Although I've often been tempted to, I have never asked a judge why he placed me as he did in more than twenty years of showing. I hope other exhibitors will do the same to me when I'm judging, although I doubt it. Most of the time I knew why I didn't place higher. Some of the times I really was puzzled.

"Poor sports who complain all the time make me sick. They act like it's the last show they'll go to in their lives. Maybe it'd be best if it was. But I figure the bad breaks and the good breaks will even out over the showing seasons. I've often received a ribbon I didn't think I deserved. And you know, I've never given one of them back!"

7 Billy Dickerson:
Out of the Ring and into the Ribbons

You'll hear it at almost every horse show. A rider comes out of the ring without a ribbon and says something to the effect of "The judge doesn't judge the horses, he judges the riders. He only gives ribbons to the professionals he may do business with. How can an amateur ever hope to win?"

What most of these infuriated horsemen usually won't admit, however, is that professionals ride better than they do, know more about training than they do, know more about showmanship than they do, and know more about feeding, conditioning, and grooming a horse than they do.

Still, an amateur can beat a professional if he tries to think like a professional, or if he just uses common sense and the one other commodity he has that the professional doesn't—time. Billy Dickerson, a young professional who shows Quarter Horses all over the major show circuit from his Pleasant Valley Farms in Macurgie, Pennsylvania, beats lots of amateurs, but he's also willing to offer advice on how they can beat him—when they have the better horse, that is.

Much of what he and I discussed while watching a Class "A" Quarter Horse show was especially applicable to Western pleasure classes. But a great deal of our talk could be applied to handling any breed of horse in any type of show.

"The first mistake the average amateur rider makes, once he gets two or three horses," Dickerson believes, "is to put up a ring to ride in. I think that's the worst mistake most riders make—riding too much in the ring.

Leading Quarter Horse trainer Billy Dickerson showing Flashy Croton, which earned superior awards in halter and Western pleasure and became a youth champion, too, for owner James Barton, Jr.

"Look at these horses in the ring now. Look at how many are boring to the center of the ring or moving sideways, with their heads pointed to the outside rail. That's caused by working against the ring rail at home. Once I get to where I can steer 'em and stop 'em, my horses never see a ring.

"Perhaps if I were specializing in training horses for other classes I might feel differently, but I think you can get along without ring riding for a pleasure horse. It takes time and miles to make a horse, and if they get most of that time and those miles in a ring, against a rail, they're going to get bored. Once you begin showing them, they'll learn enough about rings at the shows.

"Now take your average Western or English pleasure class. All forty horses in the class can walk, jog, take their leads, and lope. But what you want, speaking as a judge now, is a 'happy horse,' one with his ears up, looking interested in what he's doing. You also want your horse to be quiet, and to do that you have to stress that quietness while you're breaking him.

100

"I prefer to buy a prospective show horse as a two-year-old. I've seen an awful lot of good yearlings turn out to be disappointments later on. The breeders push the feed to them and grow them out too soon. Then they seem to fall apart, or their legs get damaged. I think, for these reasons, six weeks is the maximum you should show a yearling. And you should only do it for two purposes: to sell him or to season him.

"For Western pleasure I prefer a horse of fifteen hands to 15.2. A sixteen-hand horse may have too long a stride and be too strong-going. I like a horse with a good head and a long neck and long hip. Long hips and long necks generally mean a smooth-moving horse. A short neck and hip generally go with a short pastern. Naturally, I like a straight-legged horse—but then no one will tell you they like a crooked-legged one, will they?

"I've been fairly lucky in having some top pleasure horses like Dude's Baby Doll, Small Town Babe, Go Leo's Lady, Skip's Misty Bar, The American Dream, Red Ant's Classic, Paula Flower, Lad's Rose, Physical Ed, and Silver Deller. And for several years most of the top horses I showed were sorrels.

"That's just a quirk. Some men like blondes, some brunettes. But in the big classes in today's big shows, eye appeal is a must. Of

Billy Dickerson showing Patty Van in a reining class.

101

course, there are exceptions to every rule. Red Ant's Classic was a plain, little, ole' ugly black horse—but a good one. I'd prefer a little white on the legs or face, too.

"I like a horse with big, soft eyes. I shy away from 'pig' eyes or close-set ears—although I've seen some ugly 'boogers' that could do a lot.

"I start all my horses on a bosal, and they'll wear it from a week to a couple of months. I use a little short one that just fits on the end of the nose, and I like it snug to put the pressure on the nose, not on the chin. A big, floppy bosal tends to get the horse sore and his head up in the air.

"I like to longe a horse on the end of a line with his tack on a time or two before getting up on them. If they act 'bronk-ey' we'll pony them a lot and won't let them get their heads down.

"Of about fifty head of young horses we've broke in the last two to three years, we've only had one that really bucked. Just take your time and go at 'em quietly.

"You definitely should keep them in a pen or a ring until they're controllable—they'll stop and steer. Sometimes you get one you can't ride in a bosal—he hasn't any feeling in his nose and won't respond. Then I go to an English polo snaffle, it has a little longer shank than a 'Tom Thumb.' I put colts in a bitting rig a few times before I ride them in a bridle with a bit. I want them just to the point that when you take hold, they'll drop their heads. It's also an aid in teaching them to tuck their heads when they back. If there's one thing that'll lose you pleasure classes it's for your horse to poke up his head when he's backing.

"Generally, after sixty to ninety days of training, a colt should be broke for anyone to show. But once you get that control, get out of that ring and out into a pasture or onto a dirt road. Why? A horse moves out freely much better in a pasture than in a ring, and that's what they have to learn: to hit that pretty jog or lope, and the pasture is where they learn it. Of course I'll walk a bit to get them warmed up before I do anything.

"I probably don't ride my horses as long as many trainers. If I get them to do what I want in thirty-five or forty minutes, I put 'em up. You can ride them too much, you know. Ride a horse an hour every day and in a couple of weeks one hour won't be enough. You can get them too fit. Then, if you're hauling six horses like I do and you have to ride each an hour to quiet him down, that makes a rather long day.

102

Billy Dickerson working a young horse in his ring at Pleasant Valley Farms. But once the horse understands the basic commands, then it's out into the pasture.

"I have a big thirty-acre pasture at Pleasant Valley Farms where my pleasure horses are 'made.' I want to see them move in a straight line. Let them trot out free, don't try to control them until they slow down and find a natural way of going on their own.

"Let the horse go in straight lines, then do some gradual turns. When it comes to leads, I break them out of a trotting circle and they seem to take the right lead. You have more control of their heads that way. If you use a kick or a touch of a bat to go into a lope, you get them rushing and bulling into it. They're creatures of habit, and if you make it easy for them to learn you keep them happy, and that's what we're looking for in a pleasure horse.

"As long as there are horses, there'll be horse shows. It's just like racing. People want to beat someone else. If you plan to show a young horse, you've got to remember a young one can get bored and soured real fast. I've broken two-year-olds in March but never shown them until September because they were entered in pleasure futurities. Coral Skip was broke and showing a month later, but she was an exception.

"Once you're ready to show, you can't turn them out. You bleach out their coat, or they get kicked. Once we start showing horses we put 'em on a walker or pony them for light exercise. I know they'd be happier if we turned them out, but at that point

(Left) Billy Dickerson practicing for halter competition with Silver Deller, reserve world champion Western pleasure stallion, AQHA champion, and a superior halter and Western pleasure horse. (Right) Dickerson working with Dr. Leo Deller, a fine yearling colt sired by Silver Deller that posted eighteen wins, one grand, and two reserves in his first year of showing. Note the way Silver Deller has stamped his offspring with a blaze and white on his hind legs.

you can't take the chance. I also don't think you can show a young horse at halter and under saddle, too—not if you want to win a lot of halter points! You can't keep that good bloom on their coat if you ride them a lot.

"I don't think you can show a horse both English pleasure and Western pleasure. Go Leo's Lady was the best English pleasure horse I've ever seen, and both times she was shown Western pleasure she won, but it was a case of a judge liking a strong-going horse. You can't ask for a nice, easy jog off the bit in one class (Western) and then ask the horse to trot on out and look through the bridle (English). A few horses can do it, but not many.

"Generally you decide whether a horse should go English or Western pleasure by the way he moves and carries his head. You can get a lot done riding a horse two handed, in English, where you couldn't do it in a Western class. English pleasure is a good class for ex-racehorses, too. Of course, size has something to do with it. I think if you go into an English pleasure class with a 14.2 hand horse you're just kidding yourself.

"Once you're ready for your first show you should remember that first impressions are important. You have to get your horse used to working with other horses. We're lucky in that there's a riding school near our farm and we'll ride a youngster in some of their classes to get him used to being in a ring with other horses.

"There's quite a variety in the likes of the different horse show judges, but shows couldn't exist without judges. I don't think you should change the horse's style back and forth to try to do better for one particular judge at a show. If one judge doesn't like your horse, another one will. It'll all even out. Some riders will change

Billy Dickerson longeing a young show prospect at his Pleasant Valley Farm. It's a technique many Western breed trainers have borrowed from their counterparts in the hunter-jumper ranks.

Billy Dickerson with Johnnie Mills, an outstanding Western pleasure mare that placed second in the 1973 Quarter Horse Congress show's junior Western pleasure class, which had over two hundred entries. Johnnie Mills is owned by John Bishop VI.

Beverly Dickerson showing Studyhall, an AAA-AQHA champion stallion owned by Mrs. Hervey Kent. This versatile horse has won AQHA points in working hunter, roping, English and Western pleasure, halter, and working cowhorse.

their horses, but I'm not going to fight with one of mine.

"Now we come to the stage of being inside the ring, and here is where the amateur with an equally good pleasure horse frequently loses all hopes of beating the professional—because of his own mistakes. You can't tell me an amateur with only one or two horses hasn't the time—if he has the capability—to beat a professional with thirty-five or forty horses to take care of. An amateur has to have more time to spend with each horse than I do.

"Your horse has to know how to circle so he can get out of trouble in the ring. Many people lose pleasure classes because they can't get seen. Some horses do become a little timid in a ring with other horses, but they have to be able to move in and out of traffic.

"Many riders will be showing for the ring announcer instead of the judge. By that I mean they will try to do exactly what the announcer says exactly when he says it. A judge won't drop you way down for trotting or loping a few extra steps.

107

Sailor Bar Sandy, an outstanding gelding Billy and Bev Dickerson showed to many grand and reserve championships at halter. He then became an AQHA youth champion and an outstanding all-around show horse.

"It's the same thing when backing. We try to make our horses back fifteen to twenty steps sometimes—to do it until you're ready for them to stop. Too many horses get 'back-up spoiled,' only doing the five or six steps that most judges call for. They start to get smarter and soon are only backing two or three steps before stopping.

"I also think some amateurs have gone to extremes about this loose rein riding. Sooner or later they get too loose and then the horse stumbles because he isn't alert. I like enough contact so I don't have to move my hand more than just behind the saddle horn to collect my horse. It's that pretty picture to present to the judge. The loose, floppy rein doesn't look pretty to me.

"Some riders drill and drill to force a little slow, dinky jog when they should let the horse move as naturally as possible. A good judge can tell when the 'give-and-take' on the mouth is making a horse shorten stride.

"Sometimes an amateur's horse will miss a lead on that part of the ring behind the judge, yet he'll wind up getting marked down for it. The rider screws up his face and pulls and jerks. By then he's in front of the judge—who can tell just by the expression of the rider and horse that something went wrong. Stay cool, act like you're having a good time, and maybe when the ribbons are being passed out you will have a good time."

Concerning horse shows in general, Dickerson said "There's nothing wrong with the shows or the judges—I'd just like to see less of them. Sometimes I think we ought to eliminate the tiny ones. If you beat only six other riders in a class you really haven't proved anything. Some argue, 'Where will the "little guy" go?' But I think he still hasn't really accomplished anything by winning at a tiny show.

"One thing that might help, especially in Quarter Horse shows, would be to have more amateur-owner classes, or more nonprofessional classes. They create more interest in horse showing, and without that interest by the general public there is less of a demand for the services of the professional horseman."

8 Lewis "Spike" Holmes: Don't Be Afraid to Borrow Ideas

"East is East, and West is West, and never the twain shall meet," wrote Rudyard Kipling in his famous poem "The Ballad of East and West" in 1889.

When it comes to riding styles, many horsemen follow this adage. If they ride flat saddle they avoid anything that looks "Western" or "Cowboy," and if they straddle a stock saddle they surely don't want to be accused of "riding English."

But in the increasingly competitive world of the horse show, the smartest trainers of either riding category aren't above borrowing ideas from anyone, as long as their use will help them win.

One of them is Lewis "Spike" Holmes, Jr., of Delphi Falls, New York, one of the top Eastern trainers of Quarter Horses and Paints. He specializes in Western riding and reining classes, considered the best test of a well-trained Western horse. Spike believes that the "side pass," a term more common to classical dressage, can make the difference between first and third place in a Western riding class, and is also an important step in teaching a horse to change his leads at the lope, probably the most important ability the Western horse must possess.

Stock-saddle rider Holmes describes the side pass as "the ability of a horse to move directly sideways." He feels it makes a horse

110

look that much sharper and better-trained in Western riding classes when the horse and rider first must open a gate before going into the pattern ride of lead-changing, backing and going over a slight obstacle as the judge tries to determine the "riding qualities of gaits, change of leads, response to the rider, manners, disposition, and intelligence" of the horses performing for him.

Christilot Hanson Boylen of Canada, who placed among the top ten riders in dressage at the Munich Olympic Games in 1972, said that the Western term *side pass* is what classical riders call *leg yielding.* "It is one of the first suppling exercises we teach a young dressage horse," she explained. "You push the horse sideways with a driving aid—the outside leg behind the girth. It teaches him to move his hindquarters."

Lewis "Spike" Holmes, a Western trainer who doesn't mind borrowing English training techniques, riding Ty-Ette.

111

Holmes feels it is best to start teaching a horse to side pass from the ground, using a crop as an aide. The horse is Junior Mount. *Courtesy t. h. e. Studio; photo by Ken Schmidt.*

Holmes believes in teaching the movement to his Western horses at an early age, too. "I like to start a lot of my training from the ground with a young horse. He may have a halter or a bridle on his head when I begin. I'll lead him to a fence and turn him around so I'm facing it and it is behind him. Since we'll be going from right to left through a fence gate when we're competing (a year or so later), that's the way I'll teach him to move first.

"I take the bridle (or halter) in my right hand, take a short crop in my left hand, and push it into his right side, just behind the girth. . . . I'll change things around and start on his other side, teaching him to move to his left. If he takes just one step away from the pressure, I'll reward him with my voice or by petting him.

"One of the most important things about a horse is his attitude in trying to do what you ask. As you go along and ask more and more of him, sooner or later he's apt to say 'no' and start to resist and give you trouble. If you can avoid this—not trying to ask him to do more than he's capable of—you will have a much better horse and not risk changing his attitude from willing to unwilling.

"With the side pass, just because the horse can do three or four steps directly sideways the first day doesn't mean he should do twenty or thirty steps sideways the next day. When it comes to where I'm riding a horse at the side pass and going through a gate and the horse has gone through it for about three days and then refuses, I'd punish him. If a horse knows what he's supposed to do and doesn't do it, he should be punished; just be sure he knows what he's supposed to do first."

When Holmes begins his mounted work at the side pass he introduces the horse to the gate. He'll ride parallel to the gate, then stop in line with it, side-pass over to his left, and again stop. At this point he uses his right hand to open the latch and then rattles the gate and moves it around (while mounted or from the ground if necessary) to get the horse used to it and show him that it won't hurt him even if he bumps into it.

After the horse has lost his fear of the gate, Holmes side-passes into the opening a step or two and then lets the horse stand there. If the horse stands quietly he'll pet him, then go on through, using his left hand on the reins all the time and using only his right hand to push the gate away from him and latch it again after it swings shut. After the gate is closed, it's important to keep the horse standing there so he doesn't develop the habit of rushing through.

"I think side-passing through a gate is much more impressive than having the horse face into the gate and reaching in front of him to open the gate. I believe it can give you quite an advantage over your competitors; it's frequently the difference between first place and third. And with competition the way it is, you need every advantage you can get."

Holmes also believes that holding a horse's head in the side pass helps to get him "collected in his mouth" and teaches him to "give his head" to the rider. He starts all his horses as two-year-olds, with a medium-weight bosal hackamore adjusted for a certain amount of pressure on both nose and jaws, without being tight. The horses are started at pleasure riding, never more than thirty to forty minutes at a time, with a lot of quiet jogging through fields and pasture. Holmes will show a two-year-old in pleasure classes but believes reining, Western riding, and other more strenuous classes should be limited to three-year-olds and older horses.

When it comes to teaching a horse to take the proper lead at the

113

lope (canter), Spike Holmes insists that the most important thing is never to let a horse lope on the wrong lead. He begins by trotting a horse a few strides, using his outside leg cue and then drifting into the lope. If it's a two-year-old who gets off wrong, he'll stop, put the horse back into a trot, and ask him to lope again. But if it's a three-year-old who already knows the lope cues, he might be set back a bit by the reins, spanked with the rein ends, and started off again.

When it comes to teaching a horse to change leads, he uses a short bat or crop to cue the horse, "spanking" the horse's right flank, for instance, when going from a counterclockwise direction (or lead) into a clockwise direction. This, combined with his previous work at the side pass, gets the horse moving sideways and gets his body into the proper position to make the lead change easier and more comfortable.

Once mounted, the crop again can be used to reinforce the rider's leg aides for the side pass, as Spike Holmes is doing on Junior Mount, a son of J Bar Junior out of national champion Paint mare Lady Mount. *Courtesy t. h. e. Studio; photo by Ken Schmidt.*

114

Holmes believes a side pass through a gate in a Western riding class can mean the difference between first and third place. Here he is demonstrating on Painted Flit, an American Paint Horse Association champion. *Courtesy t. h. e. Studio; photo by Ken Schmidt*

"I'd rather use a whip cue than spurs, because spurring can get the horse rushing into the lead change and perhaps getting disunited [between his front and hind legs]," he explained. "Lope in a circle, stop, pick up the horse's head, use your whip cue. Trot a few steps if you have to, but gradually cut down on the number of trotting strides [steps] until he gets where you can check his head, stop, take one step, and then take the other lead.

"Do that until the horse gets really light in your hand. Then you can eliminate the hesitation between the cue changes. Everything depends on the horse. Don't crowd him, don't try to make him do more than he can. If he's started out right, he'll have a willing, cooperative attitude, and you don't want to lose that."

Once the horse has learned the smooth change of leads, Holmes will lope in a circle in one direction five or six times, then (going back to the trot) make a simple lead change, and then try the smooth change back in the other direction.

"Try to do it outside your ring and away from your fence," he warns. "When you feel the horse begin to anticipate the lead change, go back to pleasure riding."

Like the side pass, Holmes believes in teaching a horse to back from the ground at first. He uses a bosal on the horse's head, a voice cue and pressure on the nose to make the horse back up. If you have to tap him on the nose, you do, until the horse gets to the point where you just touch his nose with the bosal and he'll back up.

"When you're starting a horse, the first few times you can show him how to side-pass or back much easier from the ground," he emphasizes. "If you're on his back your cues are not as clear and the horse might fight you because he doesn't understand. I do very little work on the longe line or by ponying a young horse from the back of an older horse.

"I really don't think you're teaching a horse anything by longeing or ponying; you're just exercising him. If I had a rank colt that might want to buck, I might longe him to get him used to the saddle, but I don't believe in this type of training for the average colt."

When Holmes gets into mounted work in backing up, he uses a squeeze with both legs. This "squeezes" the horse up and collects him and he can back in a faster, smoother manner. Since the Western riding class requires a horse to lope over an obstacle just high enough to break his stride, such as a log, Holmes begins by walking over the log, then jogging over it, and then jogging over two or three logs in a row. This teaches the horse to watch where he puts his feet, which helps him when he moves into training for the lead changes around poles or barrels that are a major part of the class conditions.

As in the more advanced reining competition, Holmes believes it is essential not to let the young—or old—show horse perform the entire pattern. For Western riding, he sets up stakes in the training area and may weave in and out of a couple in succession, but then he'll go back into a few circles to "keep him honest."

Pattern in Gold, the fine mare he showed in the early 1970s, soon "learned where she was going, but if you feel it, try to keep the horse's attention by clucking or speaking to him. If I felt her fading closer to the stake or tree, I'd try to hold her over to the middle and speak to her. Otherwise they will lose their finesse and brush the trees. If they begin coming too close, try to stay as far

116

away from the stake or tree as you can and still keep the pattern."

When it comes to a young horse, Holmes will set up the training ring with all the stakes and obstacles the show ring class will contain and try the horse on the complete pattern three or four days before the first show in which the horse is entered. If he does it well with a minimum of trouble, he'll take him to the show.

"You'll probably have some type of problem the first few shows," said Holmes. "The strange surroundings, noise and excitement can bother a young horse, so you have to make allowances for the horse's attention wandering. If you decide to keep showing, then I would advise not riding him through the full pattern at home, just parts of it. Ride him a lot for pleasure, and work him very little on the pattern, perhaps once a week during the show season."

When it comes to the type of Quarter Horse he prefers for Western riding and reining, Spike Holmes likes the "middle of the road" type, neither too "bulldog" nor too "racey" in appearance.

Two-handed riding may be scorned by some Western trainers, but Spike Holmes finds it a fine way to get a horse to flex and give his head to the rider, as Junior Mount, only two at the time, is doing here. *Courtesy t. h. e. Studio; photo by Ken Schmidt.*

117

Jay's Cathy, who finished 28th of 146 entries in the 1976 Quarter Horse Congress Reining Futurity, shows how a top reining horse "sits down behind."

With legalized betting being permitted on Quarter Horse racing in more states, he feels Quarter Horses will continue to have a lot of Thoroughbred blood bred into them, but he doesn't want to see the abandonment of performance lines that have made the Quarter Horse so popular with youthful riders.

"If a horse has ability, size isn't important," said Holmes. "I've ridden some great big horses that didn't look like they had athletic ability, but did. And I've ridden others that looked like athletes and weren't.

"For Western riding, I like a free-moving horse with eye appeal. He should look athletic, not drafty. If you spend the time training him, he should have enough good looks to look sharp when he's finished. He should have a clean, fine throat latch with room in his throat to enable him to give his head to you.

"For reining, the horse has to have a little more ambition, a little more ability to stop and slide. Both Western riding and reining are classes that are based on athletic ability and timing, and if a horse can win consistently in Western riding, he or she usually has the ability to win in reining."

The sliding stop is taught at first from the jog. Using the voice for the cue to "whoa" and a leg squeeze will push the reining horse's legs up under him. Using protective boots is a necessity on reining horses, Holmes emphasizes.

The reining horse must be taught to lope or run freer than the controlled, slower lope of the Western riding horse. When the horse is taught to slide to a stop from the run, he will only make the long, sliding, eye-catching stop if his hind feet reach quite a bit forward underneath his body. Then, when you give him the "whoa" and leg squeeze cues, he can slide a greater distance.

Spins and roll-backs are a part of reining class patterns. Holmes teaches the spin by again going back to the English style and using one hand on each rein. The horse is ridden at the walk in smaller and smaller circles, bringing his head in and getting his front feet to cross over as he is circled. This is not done just as an exercise in itself, but is interspersed with other movements as the horse is ridden. Once in a while you should jog the horse and turn him back over his hocks.

One thing to guard against is letting the horse get "rubber-necked." He should turn his shoulders, not just his head and neck. After he is doing the work at the walk and jog well, he should be loped in a circle, stopped, and turned back—sometimes to the inside and sometimes to the outside of the circle. The outside leg should be used just behind the girth to keep the horse from swinging over. If he isn't bending well, you should use the inside leg at or a bit in front of the girth, to teach him to drop his shoulders and head.

"When you are teaching a roll-back, always stop and then turn to avoid the horse's turning in a circle," Holmes advises. "Keep him collected, stop, then turn around, then leave. Don't try to do too much too soon.

"One of the problems that can arise very quickly with a reining horse is 'scotching,' not running free for you. He gets to cheating in his circles, fading the other way, keeping his neck and front feet in the circle but letting his hind end drift out.

"If you ride at least half your time in the pasture and only half your time in the ring, you can cure some of the problem. If you run a lot of circles and do a lot of stopping and turning, when you feel the horse begin to anticipate, then it's time to do something else.

"Never let your reining horse run the complete pattern at home. You also should know that although there are four patterns listed in the American Quarter Horse Association's show rules, it is the first two they use in most shows and those are the ones you should practice. The No. 3 pattern is used a little and the No. 4

A tap with a crop can help in teaching a young horse like Junior Mount to take the proper lead at the lope. *Courtesy t. h. e. Studio; photo by Ken Schmidt.*

Michelle Holmes, eleven, shows excellent depth of heel as she rides Rapid Rapture, a three-year-old Paint who won the New York State Reining Futurity and was the state's Paint pleasure champion in 1977. *Courtesy t. h. e. Studio; photo by Ken Schmidt.*

120

pattern very rarely. I think all the patterns are good ones and fair to your horse.

"Remember," Holmes concludes, "if you keep watching other riders at a show, no matter what kind of class they are competing in, you may find something that can help you."

9 Bob Kowalewski:
The Making of a Supreme Champion

Horse-owning can be profitable. But the profit usually comes only when the horseman sells his best horse. The immediate financial gains quite often begin to pall when the replacement horse or horses fail to match the personality or winning record of the sold champion. The horseman now finds himself coming out of the show ring with a white ribbon—or no ribbon—instead of a blue.

About the only other way to make a profit and keep "the best horse I've ever owned" is to breed from him or her. The costs involved in racing horses are astronomical—but so are the rewards.

The show horse path is less costly, but there is less guarantee that showing success will be followed by breeding demand. It is quite possible to accumulate trophies and blue ribbons by the dozen simply by figuring out where the best horses are competing each weekend and then taking your trailer in the opposite direction! Far too many horses are "champions" of one region or association or breed organization, but aren't really held in high regard by knowledgeable horsemen.

One show ring designation, however, appears to guarantee its holder is a horse that must be respected: the American Quarter Horse Association's title of "Supreme Champion." To earn this title a horse must prove himself a champion of conformation close to breed perfection, a near track-record racehorse, and possessor of the "cow sense" inherited from the cowboys' choice mounts in the days long before there was a recorded Quarter Horse breed.

To become an AQHA Supreme Champion, a horse must achieve (and usually in the following order) three things:

122

Deck Jack, Supreme Champion Quarter Horse stallion owned by Robert Kowalewski of East Aurora, New York.

(1) Earn two official speed ratings of 90 or higher (or AAA time). To win a 90 rating the horse must run a race no slower than one-tenth of a second off the track record. To make sure this doesn't happen at a "no account" track populated by horses of the same designation, there are limits set. For example, at 220 yards the horse must run in :12.10 unless the track record is lower than :12.00 for the distance. Running two such races would earn the horse eight AQHA points.

(2) Win the title of Grand Champion in at least two A-rated shows under two different judges. An A-rated show must have at least 225 horses entered, which pretty much guarantees a top field of horses. The Supreme Champion must accumulate at least fifteen points at halter, which would require him to win at least three classes in his age category. In a class of twenty-five horses, the first-place winner gets five points; in a class of thirty or more entries, first place gets six points and the second-place horse gets five points.

(3) Win at least twenty-five points in performance classes, with

Deck Jack winning a race at Los Alamitos Race Course in California in 1968, going 350 yards in :18.3 seconds, AAA time. Like many Thoroughbreds, the Quarter Horse stallion became a show horse after his race career.

points coming as a result of the number of horses in a class as explained before. At least eight points must be won in reining, working cowhorse, Western pleasure, Western riding, or jumping classes (in any one or more of those classes), and eight more points must be won in calf roping, steer roping, or cutting classes (in any one or more of these classes).

It would be hard to think of any conditions to add to the AQHA's Supreme Champion rules that could further guarantee that a chosen Supreme Champion meets the breed's ideal of speed, performance, beauty, and trainability. One might force a horse to win a certain number of pleasure classes, which would seem to guarantee a quiet disposition—except that many quiet horses might not have the "eye appeal" to catch a judge's glance when in a ring with thirty or forty others.

At any rate, if a Quarter Horse can meet the stringent demands of the Supreme Champion accolade, he or she certainly should meet the knowledgeable breeder's demands, too, and guarantee his owner-breeder adequate financial compensation from the sale of his offspring. The financial demands of training and campaigning a horse for the racetrack and show ring would seem to limit those seeking such honors to stallions and mares. (At the time of this writing, most of the twenty or so Supreme Champions recognized by the AQHA are stallions.)

One who received the honor is Deck Jack, owned by Robert (Bob) Kowalewski of East Aurora, New York, who kindly explained the expenses, problems, and personal and financial rewards involved in making his horse a Supreme Champion.

Like most horse lovers, Bob became involved with horses early.

124

Bobby and Bob Kowalewski greet Deck Jack, Jr., a son of Deck Jack, in the winner's circle at Tioga Park, Nichols, New York. Rick Stark is the jockey.

He was leading ponies at picnics at twelve and at sixteen was running a rental stable of twenty horses. Then came service as a Marine Corps drill instructor during World War II, after which he moved from apprentice bricklayer to subcontractor to contractor. He is now president of a construction firm.

He built a summer home in 1964 and bought his first four Quarter Horses for trail riding. While riding with a friend on weekends, the two men began to discuss buying a top-quality stallion and—hopefully—campaigning him to become a Supreme Champion. Bob later bought a one hundred-acre farm as the future breeding location for the yet-unseen stallion.

While traveling around the country on construction business, Bob looked at "hundreds" of stallions, but few met his standards. As a matter of fact, he bid on only two in all that time. One was Deck Jack and the other was Diamond Duro, who also became a Supreme Champion. His bid on the latter had to be "no-saled" when his partner suffered a heart attack.

"In February, 1969, I went to the Indianapolis, Indiana, Speed Sale," he recalled. "I was looking for AAA speed and, as I do now, I arrived a day early to look the horses over. I personally call AQHA headquarters in Amarillo, Texas, to check on any horse I'm considering buying.

125

"Charley Champion had brought Deck Jack, then five years old, up from Oklahoma, and right away he struck me as having the conformation excellence needed to win halter points. His disposition was very docile for being off the racetrack only a short time. And his legs were blemish-free after fifty-three starts in two and a half years. In fact, his wide, flat, strong bone has drawn much attention in the show ring, and photos of his legs have been used at clinics around the nation as examples of perfect bone structure.

"I know many horses are tranquilized at sales to make them appear docile, but with Charley Champion's reputation, he couldn't afford to operate that way. In fact, Charley told me to have my son, Bobby, then twelve, go into the stall with the horse and feed and water him before the sale.

"The only other quality I investigated was Deck Jack's 'heart,' which I felt would indicate whether he would cooperate in being trained for show ring events. His racing record indicated consistently top speed every time out of the starting gate, and I felt if he could give his best so consistently on the track he would do it in the ring, too."

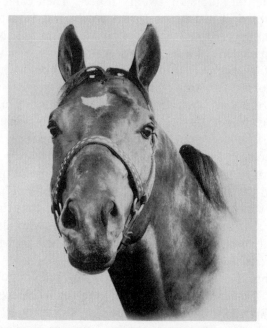

Alert head of Supreme Champion Deck Jack. The bay stallion's thin throat latch was a key factor in his purchase.

Kowalewski is proudest of the fact that he picked out the horse himself, without professional guidance. One of his reasons for buying Deck Jack was the horse's thin throat latch, which gives him the balance a good horse needs. Once he saw Deck Jack run, play, spin, and turn in a paddock, he was sure he would show that balance in the show ring.

The winning bid was only $3,900, and after the horse was bought no one came rushing up to its new owner, saying they'd come late and offering him a quick profit if he'd resell Deck Jack. This happens quite often at a sale. When it didn't, Kowalewski experienced some doubts about what he'd purchased.

Harry Hurd, a full-time dairy farmer and long a part-time professional horse trainer, soon convinced his friend he'd made a good purchase, and together they began showing Deck Jack on weekends, picking up his first points at halter.

One of the first decisions Kowalewski came to was that weekend showing would extend the time needed to make Deck Jack a Supreme Champion, so he contacted Billy Dickerson, a full-time professional from Pennsylvania, who had admired the

Beverly Dickerson showing Deck Jack in a Quarter Horse English pleasure class at the Erie County Fair in Hamburg, New York.

127

bay stallion at a show. Billy was able to go to far more shows and quickly gained enough halter and English pleasure points to make Deck Jack an AQHA Champion, which required thirty-five show points in five different shows and under five different judges, with fifteen won at halter and fifteen in performance—eight points in each category to be won at "A" or "B" (one hundred fifty to two hundred twenty-four entries) shows.

With a 15.3-hand frame, it was obvious that Deck Jack would be best in English pleasure. He was not a "pokey" horse and his long stride made it hard for him to move slow enough to place in Western pleasure. But English pleasure was just right for the ex-racehorse, and he soon had eleven points after only four shows. After the 1970 breeding season, weekend showing added another thirty halter points and eight show grand champion stallion trophies.

By the fall of 1970 all that was needed were the eight points in roping or cutting, and trainer Roy Savage of Durant, Oklahoma, had been chosen to train Deck Jack for roping. Savage has done the same "finishing off" for at least four other Supreme Champions. But then came the VEE outbreak, and Deck Jack wasn't shipped to the Southwest until the fall of 1971.

Of course, Kowalewski had confided his Supreme Champion hopes to Dickerson, and while Billy was showing the horse in pleasure he also was teaching him quick stops and turns to make it easier for Savage to train him for roping.

During this time, it was not a case of everything going out in training, entry and shipping expenses and nothing coming in except trophies, ribbons, and a few dollars in prize money. Deck Jack was bred to around fifty mares in 1970 and 1971, at a $300 stud fee.

"The first year we had good mares, but not of really outstanding quality," Kowalewski recalled. "The next year, with one crop of foals on the ground, we got better mares.

"In 1972, with two crops of foals available for inspection, we bred the same number of mares at a fee of $400, but they were of really top quality. In 1973, with a fee of $750, we had the same number of mares to be bred, but this time they were of super quality, and represented many of the top breeders in the business.

"If Deck Jack could get decent colts out of the mares he'd had in the past, he should get really top colts out of the new mares."

During Deck Jack's first years at stud, Kowalewski gave free

Top roping trainer Roy Savage roping a calf from Deck Jack, then in training at Roy's ranch in Durant, Oklahoma. Savage has "finished off" several AQHA Supreme Champions.

stud services to mares who had achieved an AAA record as runners or who had produced foals that made an AAA speed mark. The stud fee was cut fifty percent for mares with AA ratings or production records.

"The real money is on the racetrack," Kowalewski admitted. "We felt we had to get some good running horses to the races right away. Then, when they produce, the mares will be coming up to New York from Texas and Oklahoma."

But these big plans still were in the incubator stage when Deck Jack made his trip to Roy Savage's ranch to be trained for roping—to learn to turn his racing speed on and off at the slightest cue from his rider, to come to a hard stop and back off to hold the calf still for tying.

"When I sent Jack to Roy Savage," said Bob, "I was sure he'd have to work the horse so hard, because of his race breeding, that he'd soon be skin and bones. I really was shocked when I saw him in February 1972, at the big Denver Fat Stock Show. I could hardly recognize him for his bloom and the fact he was carrying more weight than ever before."

The finished product wasn't that easy in the making. Savage admitted to many a sleepless night wondering if the big bay stud ever would differentiate between a racetrack starting gate and a calf roping box. The first time he was backed into the wood-fenced roping area next to where calves break out of a chute, Deck Jack thought he was in a starting gate and came barreling out in AAA time—going right past the calf!

Savage began walking him into the box, and then walking him right back out. Finally Deck Jack realized what was required—breaking out at the same speed as the calf and putting his rider in a proper position to rope. Once he finally ran a calf correctly, he showed the same consistency in this phase of competition as he had on the racetrack and in the show ring.

He placed consistently in every class on the early spring show/rodeo circuit, but still lacked one point of reaching the total needed for Supreme Champion.

Once again, the stallion's wonderful disposition aided his quest. He was bred from March 1 to April 15 in New York state and had absolutely no roping practice. Then his owner took him to a show in New Jersey. Savage flew up, rode Deck Jack for an hour, declared "He's ready to go," and went into the arena and won a roping event worth three points.

"That was the only secret to working this horse," said Kowalewski, "riding him an hour the morning he was to rope or an hour or two before he was to show in a pleasure class. My son Bobby or I was able to do most of the riding at a show prior to competition."

With twelve points in roping, which placed Deck Jack in the AQHA's top five for most of the 1972 show season, Deck Jack also had twenty-eight grand or reserve show championships, forty-four halter points, fifty-five reining points, and twenty-three English and Western pleasure points—probably one of the highest totals of any Supreme Champion.

"I estimate I spent $25,000 in making the horse a Supreme Champion," his owner declared. "But I thought he would be bred to at least fifty mares each year beginning in 1973 at a $750 fee and thus earn about $37,000 a year for the next ten or twelve years. Then, too, I am breeding him to my own five mares and I am able to sell the foals for much higher prices [one for $3,500].

"I had had him insured for $20,000, but after figuring everything out, I increased it to $100,000. I know I wouldn't sell him for $100,000."

A proud owner, Bob Kowalewski, accepting the AQHA Supreme Champion plaque for Deck Jack from Bud Ferber, AQHA president in 1973.

With Deck Jack's oldest foals already winning classes in Eastern show rings, Kowalewski seems well on his way to realizing a 10-to-1 return on the $30,000 he invested in his horse.

And for those interested in following his path to show ring and financial success, he offers this advice on today's breeding trends in the Quarter Horse industry:

"With more states legalizing pari-mutuel Quarter Horse racing, there are going to be more race-bred Quarter Horses produced. Yet if we breed for proper conformation, disposition, and athletic ability along with speed, we still will have a horse that can win in the show ring in halter or performance classes. This is very common with Thoroughbreds who become hunters and jumpers ridden by riders—many under 18 years—in English horse shows after being on the racetrack.

The handsome and versatile Supreme Champion Deck Jack.

"As far as size, I feel ability comes in all sizes. If you look at the size of the youngsters in junior high and high school you can see we have to have larger horses to carry them and make a good picture for the show ring judge.

"Of course, this emphasis on size and speed means more and more Thoroughbred blood in the Quarter Horse, which may be one reason that English pleasure classes are bigger than Western pleasure classes in most shows. But as a breeder you have to go along with what the public is demanding.

"Conformation and speed breeding give you the top price now and that's what you have to aim for. If you have both in a colt you can make him a successful stud even if he doesn't become a great racehorse himself, because the race breeding will show itself eventually.

"As a new breeder I have tried very hard to be fair to those who send their mares to Deck Jack. If a mare aborts or a foal dies and the owner's vet checks it out, we rebreed the mare. It is costly to truck a mare, board her, and pay a $750 stud fee, and we want to do what is right by our customers."

The Supreme Champion path to financial success probably could be followed—although the path is less clearly marked—by

Deck Jack at owner Bob Kowalewski's Deck Jack Farms in East Aurora, New York. The fine hind leg muscling of the champion stallion is emphasized in this photo.

Three weanlings in the pastures of Deck Jack Farms show the uniform white star markings that are a trademark of the stallion.

133

owners of Appaloosas or Arabians who have horses of superior conformation who are also top performers under saddle. When it comes to hunters and jumpers, the situation is more difficult. Most horses in these classes are Thoroughbreds who were gelded at an early age.

Most hunter-jumper trainers feel stallions are too much trouble on the show circuit. The A-rated shows most often use flimsy, temporary stalls during their two to five days of activity, and they would hardly hold a stallion near a mare in heat. However, an amateur did campaign Captain Flash, a stud, to top hunter honors, including a championship in Madison Square Garden. And one of the U.S. Equestrian Team's top international jumpers a few years ago was Frank Chapot's clever little gray stallion Good Twist.

So, no matter what breed of horse you own, if you have the determination and he has the ability to stand above his rivals you may be able to enjoy both financial rewards and the continued ownership of a superchampion.

10 Preparing for Showing: My First Horse

"I think I've got a horse for you."

When John Shaffner uttered those words in the fall of 1968 no bells rang or fireworks went off in my head, but they should have. After being a horse lover since the age of eight or nine I finally had reached my goal: a horse of my own. Like so many other youngsters I had been horse-crazy from an early age and grew up on Hopalong Cassidy and Gene Autry movies, a copy of C. W. Anderson's new book every year, and rides on amusement park ponies.

I had nurtured this love by working in stables during the summers of my college years and even finding horses to ride while stationed in Korea with the Army in 1953-54. I had met John Shaffner while covering horse shows in the Buffalo area for the newspaper that employed me. John had given me an introduction to fox-hunting and had allowed me to exercise and school some of his own horses, or those owned by riders who were on vacation.

"John, this is great for you," I told him one day. "I keep these horses of yours exercised and obedient while you're away at shows, then you sell them and make the profit. Why don't you find me a horse, I'll train him (with your help), and when he's sold I'll make the profit!"

Shortly afterwards Shaffner bought two horses bred by Canada's leading breeder, Edward P. Taylor. One of them was Stability, a big, bay three-year-old gelding by Stratus. Stratus had raced at two and three in Ireland and later won two handicaps on the turf in this country. He was by English Derby winner Nimbus.

Sue Thorne and Stability ready to compete in a show at Hurdle Hill Farm. *Photo by the author.*

The colt's dam, Blen Lark by Blenheim II, had produced as her first foal Blue Light, who had won the Queen's Plate, Canada's "derby." All of her other offspring, to illustrate the vagaries of Thoroughbred breeding, had won races, but none were stakes horses.

Stability was foaled June 2, 1965, Blen Lark having been bred to Stratus after slipping a cover by Choperion, a son of Chop Chop, a relatively obscure chaser of Count Fleet who went on to become a standout sire in Canada.

This horse was a perfect hunter prospect: good looking, about 16.3 in height, an athletic mover, young. Shaffner showed him to several prospective purchasers. He was away at a show when one approached him and finalized the purchase. The green-broke youngster, who had never been over a fence with a rider on his back, was sold for $6,500. (Proven show ring champions bring from $20,000 to $50,000 or more.)

When Shaffner called back to Lockport to tell his stable manager not to show the horse to anyone, he was greeted with the

Stability and Sue Thorne competing in a green hunter class in 1970. *Photo by the author.*

unhappy news that Stability had torn open his knee while out in a field. No one ever was able to figure out if he suffered the injury on a fence post, a rock, or whatever. The wound was cleaned, hosed, treated by a top veterinarian. The result was the formation of a half-inch or more of scar tissue, a "big knee" that limited flexion in the leg, and a horse that would not pass a veterinarian's inspection for soundness.

This was Stability, soon to be known as "Billy," my first horse.

First impression, first ride. A sunny Sunday in October. Someone else had ridden him, or he had been turned out, that morning. I tacked him up, took him out into the ring. He moved nicely, if a little awkwardly and "wander-y." He had nice gaits, a good mouth. He seemed friendly. I bought him.

Now, the problems involved with training a young Thorough-bred began to arise. Like most adults I worked a 10 A.M. to 6:30 P.M. day, Monday through Friday. I had three young children. Jeffrey, then seven, was in his first year of organized hockey. As a proud father, I had to be at the games on Sunday mornings. Right

Stability, ridden by Sue Thorne, competing in a horsemanship class in the bay colt's first show. *Photo by the author.*

away I was at a disadvantage. A young horse of any breed needs regular riding. I couldn't give it to Billy.

In the fall, it was not too bad. He was quiet enough so that better riders could work him when I wasn't there. He could be turned out to romp or longed before I rode him. But when winter came, difficulties mounted. He couldn't be turned out in the snow. He couldn't always be longed in the indoor arena because there might be beginners taking lessons at one end, or other riders working spooky horses.

Billy wasn't mean. He was just young, well-bred, frisky—and underexercised. And since he was my first horse, I was happy to excuse these minor defects in his not adapting himself to an infrequent, mainly weekend, training schedule. That he was able to come through such a training program unscathed is more a tribute to his good sense than to my ability as a horseman.

One of the first winter exercises to be learned was humility. Not for Billy, for Harlan. Supple teenagers whose first horses I had to work "down" before shows in past years now had to return the favor—they had to get up on Billy and keep him moving until he

The small hunt course at Hurdle Hill Farm, where I spent many hours training my first horse, Stability. *Courtesy t. h. e. Studio; photo by Ken Schmidt.*

settled down enough for me to climb aboard. As the old adage says, "Pride goeth before a (possible) fall."

Sometimes they weren't available, and I had to turn bronco-buster myself. I well remember getting up on Billy and having him go straight up on his hind legs—just once, thankfully. A friend had accompanied me to the indoor arena, and after the workout was over he gave me a compliment: "That was beautiful, just like in the movies. Why didn't you have him rear up like that again?"

Of course, there were more good times than bad. After a few circles of the ring Billy usually was ready to get to work. One possible mistake I made at first was letting him make those circles at a very collected canter. It was so slow and smooth I didn't realize he was just practicing "going to the post" at the racetrack, and that he was conserving his energy for some tomfoolery later on.

This usually took place coming around the corner of the arena and heading into a straight stretch. There was no warning, no quickening of the controlled canter. Suddenly, down would go his head, out would go his hind legs in a joyful little buck, and off he'd shoot at racing speed for a few strides. Then I'd somehow screw myself back down into the saddle and he'd usually come back under control without my touching the reins at all.

Another problem was caused by Stability's simple lack of

The author schooling Stability, a half-brother to Blue Light, winner of Canada's historic Queen's Plate, in the indoor arena at Hurdle Hill Farm, Lockport, New York.

reining "handle," combined with his lack of exercise. He had this annoying habit—when making a circle to the right, for instance—of somehow drifting out to the left, sort of bulling away from the direction in which he was pointed. But these were minor problems, really. All I had to do was get him settled down by turning him loose, longeing him, or having him ridden by a better rider, and Billy was a perfect gentleman.

Since Billy was being turned out in the arena or outdoor show ring or one of the several paddocks at Hurdle Hill so often, I began using a strategy that may horrify the horse training purists but that worked wonderfully for me. I bribed him to come to me. When I could tell he was done bucking, racing, and romping by simply observing him go from a mad gallop to a far-reaching trot, I would go into the ring, stretch out my hand, and call "Come here, Billy." When he got close there'd be a lump of sugar on my fingertips. He was never a problem to catch.

I used the same treat in his stall. A seventeen-hand horse (he grew!) can be a problem to bridle. But not if every time you put the bit in his mouth you also pushed a sugar lump against his teeth. Billy got so ingrained in this habit that all you had to do, eventually, was come into his stall with a bridle and he'd hang his handsome head right over your shoulder and down to waist height, and even open his mouth up wide. (What a trainer I was! What a sugar-lover he was!)

The first few months I owned Billy I did little more than ride him at a walk, the brisk trot he seemed to favor, and a moderate or slow canter. He had to get accustomed to carrying 190 pounds, he needed to be able to stretch his neck, to find his best point of balance. There was no sense trying to get him "on the bit" or into any type of collection. I let him go his own way as much as possible when it came to the speed of his gait. All I wanted him to do was go where I pointed him, to follow his nose.

Another problem that arose at this time concerned canter leads. Most Thoroughbreds trained for racing (I never was able to find out just how much race training Billy had had; he'd been tattooed but never had started) take their left lead more readily, since they are worked in the racetrack's counterclockwise direction so constantly. Perhaps it was a remembrance of his sire's racing in England, where they run clockwise, but Billy would take his left lead faultlessly, and get wrong when going the other direction.

I probably was contributing to the problem by anticipating his mistake and getting my weight forward so I could look down at his shoulders and see which one was leading. Trotting him into a corner and swinging into the canter at that point was one answer. Shaffner provided another, the best one: "Point him diagonally toward the wall, use your inside hand and leg (closest to the arena wall). He can't go into the wall, so he'll take the correct lead." He did.

This first winter, with Billy heading toward his fourth birthday, we did almost no jumping. Once when he'd flipped me and Shaffner had to take over, John drained some of Billy's energy by taking him over crossed rails about twenty inches high. But outside of that, there was just an occasional trot over a cavalletti series until the ride was over. While cooling him out indoors, I began my long-distance planning for the days when Billy and I would be dominating handy hunter classes, especially the ones where you had to jump a fence, dismount, then lead your mount over another fence.

Near the end of our cooling-off walk, I'd find a low rail, cluck to Billy, jump the fence myself, and Billy would follow—right into my outstretched hand and his usual sugar lump. He never refused while I was on the ground. I was hoping this pleasant habit would remain once I began jumping him while on his back, whenever that would be.

That spring and summer there was a gradual continuation of the slow schooling, this time moving to the outdoor show ring. Billy would be turned out to buck and play for ten minutes or so, and then I'd climb aboard. A good brisk trot around the ring a time or two, then a circle through the middle to divide the ring into a smaller working area, then a series of medium-sized circles, then trotting the width of the ring and changing directions right or left when we neared the rail—serpentines, which Billy quickly learned to anticipate.

The canter work was even less demanding. I always was careful to work him equally on both leads. I tried not to canter around the entire ring—about three hundred by one hundred fifty feet—too often. "Keep the circles smaller, don't let him get the idea of stretching out at speed," Shaffner kept reminding me.

Billy was easily distracted. Another horse led out of the stable or one turned out in a paddock would quickly attract his attention. He'd generally keep on with what he was doing, he'd rarely stop and stare. He'd just notice. He'd notice horses, flapping

142

coolers, children on bicycles or motor scooters, dogs rustling in high grass—just about anything. And react with a quick sideways jump that either kept me on my toes (mentally) or on my breeches on the ground (physically).

After a good workout in the ring of thirty-five to forty-five minutes, I'd take Billy out to the hunter course for a calming walk around. Later on I'd work him at the trot or canter outside the ring, but only after I was sure he'd gotten all his playfulness out of his system. I also took him outside the barn when shows were being held, to let him look at all the strange goings-on.

By now Billy was moving much more easily under me and was able to follow my leg squeezes into a faster or slower trot, a stronger canter, or a hand gallop. I quickly learned that if I used my heels to signal a hand gallop he'd generally respond with that old low-head, quick-buck routine. It was much smoother to squeeze and give a tongue cluck.

Our second winter together was a little easier. Billy was not quite so slow to settle down to business, but he still had his little idosyncrasies. The sliding door might set him off, or it might not. My children's footsteps, running through the spectator area, might frighten him—or they might not. One never knew what to expect.

We were working steadily over low fences. Depending on his mood, he might pay attention to the fence or he might spend more time looking at the instructor (Shaffner or Ed Lane) standing nearby. He might notice them at the last minute, and run out. But we were learning, we were adjusting to each other, and making progress.

The next year, his fifth, he made his show debut. He was pinned in some under saddle and equitation classes. I was announcing and one of Hurdle Hill's good young riders, Sue Thorne, rode him. Over fences he went around greenly, not folding up his knees well, according to the judge. It was a local, unrecognized show, but it was good experience.

There was more riding out on the hunt course and through the fields. For a Thoroughbred, Stability was remarkably stable once he had settled down. He could canter down a field and never get "on the bit," never get impatient with a controlled pace and want to race. He was schooled around the hunt course by the better riders. By now my sons were keeping me even busier through participation in little league football, with practices beginning early in August, hockey, and baseball.

Although I longed to ride Billy over the hunt course, Shaffner cautioned me: "You're not riding often enough (two or three times a week) to be really tight in the saddle. Low fences, fine. But you're not riding well enough to go over the hunt course." Although I agreed with reluctance, the bitter fact is that for the duration of my ownership of Billy the Lovable, roughly four years, I never did ride him over the hunt course, nor any portion of it.

That winter, however, he was a changed character. He might be a little frisky at first. But after a good workout and a few low fences I could put either Jeffrey, then ten, or Steven, then seven, up on him. Billy would walk around the indoor arena with barely a glance at other horses or riders. They could even jump a fence as he was walking past the jump standards and it wouldn't faze him. He would calmly walk around in the center of the outdoor show ring while I instructed Jeff and Steve on their mounts from the lesson horse string.

I could easily have shown him that summer, but too often I was involved with being a show announcer or show steward. So he had to stay in the barn, or just watch the show between mouthfuls of grass.

The next winter, as he was approaching his eighth birthday, was the beginning of the end. One of the Hurdle Hill lesson riders showed him to several ribbons against fairly good competition. The stable began scheduling shows for those who were taking lessons or not otherwise showing regularly. Jeff, riding a fourteen-hand brown-and-white pony, and I won the "parent-child, walk-trot" class at the first one, for one of my most enjoyable equestrian experiences ever. In fact, that class proved so popular that more parents and children entered than there were horses available. Stewart Moran, the head instructor, even borrowed Billy (the rearer) for another parent to use in a second parent-child class. She couldn't even get him to trot!

I rode him in an open show, finally, and won a ribbon in every class on the flat in which we showed. I was envisioning a summer of occasional showing, a fall of fox hunting—but John Shaffner brought an end to the reverie. "You know, he's really a 'made' horse now," he said one day. "He's a good hack, he can jump a course. You either ought to start showing him regularly, start Jeff showing him—or sell him."

What a dilemma! I really couldn't afford to show him myself.

Sherry Krafjack riding Stability in a horse show at Blue Ribbon Farms, Northbrook, Illinois.

Jeff was so involved with school, football, hockey, and baseball that he hardly had a minute to relax. My wife was in so many car pools she surely would rebel if schooling sessions for Jeff and Billy were added. Reluctantly, I came to the only logical conclusion. It was stupid to keep a horse for occasional pleasure riding that was capable of doing so much more. It might be best for Billy to bring home show ring ribbons for someone else.

And, of course, he did just that. Stability was bought by Rickey Harris, operator of Stonehedge Farm, in Libertyville, Illinois. That summer, when Shaffner took his show string to the big "A"-rated shows in Chicago, there was Stability, fat and sassy, placing fourth in a green working hunter under-saddle class against really top horses, winning a junior hunter under-saddle class, and placing third in a junior hunter over-fences class at the Blue Ribbon show and placing third in the junior hunter under-saddle class at the next week's Grand National show.

That winter, at the Chicago International Hunter and Jumper Show, believed the largest show of its type in the Chicago area's history, Billy won the junior hunter under-saddle class. At a similar show in January, he placed fourth in the open working hunter under-saddle class. Later in 1974 he was sold to Sherry

Krafjack of Racine, Wisconsin, and he continued his ribbon-winning ways.

No matter how many horses I will own in the future, I doubt if any of them will replace big, goofy, spooky, lovable Billy in my memories and affections.

11 A Nightmare Evaporates: The Hans Renz Clinic

My horse was plunging and dancing, sweat glistening on his neck and slithering through my fingers as I patted him, trying to calm him down. Watching, nervous snickers betraying their own apprehension, were several teenagers astride groomed-to-perfection and calm horses. Ahead loomed an unbelievable combination of fences and a ramrod-stiff instructor rasping: "Herr Abbey, you vill engage your horzes' hocks beneeze you and you vill jump the three-foot szpread, szhorten stride, and jump out over the five foot oxer."

"No, no, I can't—I've never jumped anything higher than three and a half feet. I can't—I won't—I, I, I—". I awoke in a tangle of bedclothes, with my wife annoyingly asking, "Another bad dream about the Hans Renz clinic?" "No, nothing like that," I mumbled. "Go back to sleep."

Too bad I couldn't follow my own advice. Because, of course, it was the approaching two-day clinic that was once again causing me to worry about my horse and my horsemanship. I really didn't know too much about Hans Renz, who was to teach that clinic at Hurdle Hill Farm in March, 1973, but with a name like that he had to be German. And everyone knows how the German school of horsemanship regards the horse as a four-footed machine that must unhesitatingly follow the rider's every dictate.

A little closer investigation revealed that Mr. Renz had coached the Canadian Three-Day Event Team in Mexico in 1968, which did little to ease my anxiety. Everyone remembers how it rained in Mexico during the 1968 Olympic Games, turning the cross-country course into a quagmire, resulting in fatal injuries to at

147

A smiling group of riders are introduced to three-day event trainer Hans Renz by John Shaffner prior to a memorable clinic at Hurdle Hill Farm in 1973.

least two horses. Anyone who could coach a team to get all four of its riders over a course like that had to be a rather stern taskmaster!

But, of course, the real problem for me was that I was that much-despised commodity: the weekend rider! With a young, active family and a nonriding wife, it had been hard to get away to Hurdle Hill often enough to do a really proper job of making over a three-year-old Thoroughbred into a dependable family mount. It wasn't until "Billy" was "coming seven" that I could trust him to carry Jeff (then ten) or Steven (seven), and it wasn't until the winter of 1972-73 that any little distraction would not cause him to run out or stop at a jump.

So I felt fairly confident that he would be able to handle any of the indoor arena jumping courses. But whether I'd be able to was another story.

Hans Renz, as he began his introduction to the clinic, was a pleasant surprise. No razor-cleared sideburns or Prussian monocle, no slapping of gloves or crop on his boots to make a point. (Maybe he was just putting me off my guard?)

148

"The driving seat is my 'bag,' " he began. "Moving your horse with your seat is easier than using your strength. It makes it easier for both horse and rider." Hans was born in Germany, but moved to Switzerland at the age of seventeen and competed on that nation's dressage team on the international level, winning classes at Munich and Frankfort with the well-known horse Olymp.

Later, he became a professional and trained in Switzerland for fifteen years, then went to Ireland, where his pupils included Olympic rider Jessica Fowler. He also trained the Swiss junior three-day-event team. Renz came to Canada in December 1967 to coach its three-day-event team and had been coaching all over North America ever since.

"The better you sit, the softer your aids can work," he went on. "When going around the ring, you should see the horse's inside eyeball. Don't push your whole heel down; that stiffens your leg. You collect your horse into a compressed spring, restraining in front but pushing stronger from the seat. Your seat slows the canter down, you're not pulling him down.

"The inside rein supples, the outside rein (nearest the arena's walls) guides. The inside rein should just be a slight vibration

Hans Rens uses some "body Austrian" to demonstrate the driving seat he advocates.

149

because if you have three pounds of pressure on your inside rein, you must double that force on the outside rein. This stronger force is more tiring for both horse and rider. But if your inside rein is vibrating with only two or three ounces of pressure, then your outside rein can get results with only one pound of pressure, and you'll need only one pound of driving force from your seat."

My head was beginning to swim and I regretted not having a slide rule handy when Hans added, "Also, stronger inside pressure automatically pushes the horse's hindquarters out. If you let the horse escape behind your legs, you lose your spring. The hindquarters must always follow the track the front legs make and the horse must bend from head to tail, around your inside leg. The duty of the legs is to keep his hindquarters framed. You bend the horse around your leg not by pushing with that inside leg—that can only push the hindquarters out.

"Ninety-nine percent of all riders try to turn right by pulling the inside rein, which automatically turns the hindquarters out. Instead it should be the inside rein playing 'a soft tune' and the outside rein pushing harder. This is the way the United States Equestrian Team and everyone in Europe works, the way Rodney Jenkins rides. You will never see their horses going around a turn with their heads bent to the outside.

"It's show and let go, show and let go—otherwise you can't make short turns and your spring is weakened. The horse will learn you don't have to hold him and hang onto him. Then, after a correct turn, all you will need are two straight strides before a fence. If you lose the horse's impulsion through your turn, you lose your spring. If you get more speed, then you need four or five strides to get straight and get compressed.

"So if you turn sharper you will get easier timing to your fences, and most riders—and horses—have a better 'eye' for stride adjustment at closer distances than from several strides away."

Now it was time to put the lecture theory into practice. The first group of riders were John Shaffner's regular show string, on their ribbon-winning mounts. Renz worked them on the sitting trot, lengthening and shortening strides in a circle, and then on striking off into the canter. "Bring the forehand in front of the hindquarters, and at the moment he is straight use your seat in a sideways push toward his inside foreleg." It worked—for them.

Now it was time for his first jumping exercise, the "Box and Walls." This was four jumps in a square at one end of the indoor

150

arena. The rails were eighteen inches high to start. It was an in-and-out jumping exercise, but Hans didn't describe it that way.

"This is not a jumping exercise, this is a turning exercise. I like this for a young horse. He can't start running because the walls won't let him. So you don't have to get rough with your hands to turn him. He learns to look after himself and to keep listening to you so he'll know which way to turn."

But the well-trained show horses didn't seem to catch onto the idea too quickly. There were a few refusals, some hurried, stiff jumps, a couple of rails down before the rhythm of the exercise took hold.

When it came time for the second group to ride, my nerves began to get tense once again. My first problem came when I rode up to the instructor and asked, "How are my stirrups?" and he replied, "shiney." But before I could become more flustered, he gathered our group together to explain: "For dressage, for schooling on the flat, your stirrup must be long enough so that by just picking up your toe—with your leg in a comfortable

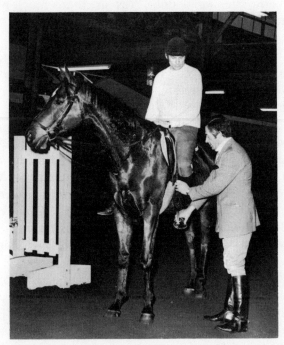

Hans Renz and I work out a problem in proper stirrup length as Stability considers the situation.

151

position—you are able to put your foot into your irons." (For me, this was four holes longer than I had been riding.) For equitation work, you should shorten two holes, and for jumping one or two more."

Hans then showed me, a 190-pound six footer who naturally stretches his near side stirrup leather quite a bit, an easy way to check stirrup length. You fold your iron back up (so the tread points in the air) from the end of your leather and measure with your fingers from the top of the tread to the bottom of your saddle flap. "Leathers stretch; flaps don't," he explained.

Then it was into that horrible sitting trot. I'd done some sitting trot work before, of course—hasn't everyone? But it had always been sitting on a nice, short-moving horse. I'd never tried it on my seventeen-hand, long-striding Stability. Hans Renz made it look so easy—so how come I was bouncing all over the place? How come I had to lean back until my head was practically touching his tail until I could feel in some sort of rhythm?

A consultation with "Dr." Renz seemed in order. He quickly diagnosed my ailment: my horse was trotting too fast. I had to soften and slow him up. I did. "Yes sir, that's much better." A word of praise. Ah, ha! I glowed. Just let me at the "Box and Walls."

Then it was time. "Who's going to go first?" I steeled myself. Was my bad dream going to come true? Would I be the object of derision? Well, I told myself, why wait—forward!

And what do you know? Good old "Billy" trotted strongly up to the box, popped over the first rail, leaped over the second, I remembered to flex my inside rein and push with the outside rein and—lo and behold! We were dancing! It was trot, up, and over; stride, turn, up and over; turn and trot and jump again. With very little push from my seat Billy soon was cantering, turning, and leaping like a stag. It was great. A star rider was born!—Well, I was a star until the next rider did the exercise just as well (all right, almost as well) as "Billy" and I. And so ended Day Number One of the Hans Renz clinic.

The next day, both groups met with our instructor for some more "chalk talk" before riding. We had lots of questions.

"There are two different ways of schooling horses," Hans Renz told us. "You can frighten him by beating him if he stops at a fence. I am apalled to see even properly trained riders do this all too frequently. But a day always comes when they come in

152

Hans Renz advocates adjusting stirrup length in relation to the bottom of the saddle flap, and I follow his instructions, hoping it will help.

wrong—especially to a spread—and then they say 'No.' Amateurs shouldn't beat or be rough. I don't mind a horse stopping, unless it's a fence he's jumped twenty times before. But if he's young and it's a new type of fence, he shouldn't feel pain.

"Build his confidence. Be consistent with your aids. Don't jump four feet before he can jump three feet really well—don't ask him 'stupid questions' he can't 'answer' or that will hurt him. If you're a professional and you have a rough one who's stopped with every other rider and the owner can't afford a year's training bills to remake him—that's a different thing.

"Now let's talk about hands. Who has the harder hand, a three-hundred-pound man or a six-year-old child? The answer is the child. A loose, snatching rein is more painful than a steady, heavy pull.

153

"Equipment? The thicker a bit, the softer it is. Racing D or wire snaffles are harder bits and make it difficult to push the horse up into them. This is 'stepping on coals' in the United States but hack classes, with horses performing on loose reins, automatically brought in the wire snaffle. You may beat the showing system, but you're not schooling correctly.

"Of course, there's 'system beating' in every type of competition. When I was showing in dressage, the way we would try to make a dry-mouthed dressage horse look good was to put soap powder in his mouth. Then it looked like he was soft-mouthed and chomping on his bits, as a properly trained horse should do.

"Short martingales and running reins bring pressure from below and pull the head down. This doesn't improve the muscle at the top of the horse's neck, which helps him flex. So as far as I'm concerned those pieces of equipment are absolutely useless. They only teach a horse not to raise his head—they don't do anything to bring his hind legs under him. Side reins fixed to the girth are all right and the French 'chambot' working on the top of his head helps to form the muscle on the top of his neck and is permissible.

"I have to admit I prefer horse trials or combined training events to showing. It's not so businesslike. I think the people competing are more relaxed and have more fun. I think it is a coming sport and as more people participate they will become more interested in dressage, which will help that phase of riding.

"When it comes to the proper tack for eventing—the egg-butt snaffle bit looks smart for shows, but the rings don't go completely through the bit so it is hard to tell how worn they are. So they break! It happens hundreds of times on the cross-country phase—not just once. It is the same with rubber-covered reins. Most saddlery firms use two pieces of rein stitched together inside the rubber covering. So they weaken and break. It has happened twice to Canadian team members. I'd advise buying a good set of leather reins, in one piece, and then have them covered with rubber. When it comes to stirrups, 'show irons' are nice and shiney, but very easy to break, especially on the cross-country phase. The 'old-fashioned' type are heavier. They'll bend but won't break, and they are easier to pick up if you lose them."

Now it was time to review yesterday's work and begin today's exercises.

"Today we'll play some rather interesting games. We'll have little fences and we'll ride them like they were four feet high—to

154

"He sure makes it look easy," I think, as Hans Renz floats past at a perfect sitting trot.

prove whether our horses are sufficiently schooled on the flat. We want good turns and timing. You'll be both lengthening and collecting your horse. It's too late when you approach a fence and have to push with your seat ten times before he answers you with an increase in pace. He has to answer you the first time. And the push is from your hips down, not from your head and down."

This low spread doesn't look like much now, but after ninety minutes of hard work it appeared as wide as the Grand Canyon to me—and Stability seemed to agree, at first.

In this exercise we had two fences down each side of the arena. We were to ride the first pair with four strides between and the second with five strides between them—then gradually lengthen our horses' strides so the second time we were doing the combinations in three and four strides, respectively. Stability did it perfectly, and once again I received a "Not bad, sir." Welcome words indeed.

Then it was time for a new lesson.

"For sharper turns, you need to use a half- or quarter-pirouette, which is simply another aid to stop the horse's hindquarters from drifting out. To keep him in the proper rhythm, you push your weight to the inside—push down with your foot, don't collapse the inside hip by bending at the waist. The outside hand brings the forehand in, assisted by the outside leg. The inside leg prevents a shift of the horse's body. The inside rein works very softly.

"This is a dressage aid, but it's very successful in jumping. Again, Rodney Jenkins is the prime example. And this is harder to practice at the walk, when the horse has three feet on the ground, than it is at the canter, when his weight is suspended."

Once again it was practice, and then apply. And no one seemed to have any trouble with it. Finally, it was time for the last

156

jumping exercise, taking a small spread in the middle of the ring. Since we first had mounted, it had been about ninety minutes of riding and jumping interspersed with short lectures. For me, the time had sped by much too swiftly. For Stability, unbeknownst to me, it wasn't the same. Ninety minutes was one and a half hours, about thirty to forty minutes more exercise, and more strenuous exercise at that, than he was used to.

So when it came time to tackle the spread, which looked imposing even to me, he refused! Then refused again, before I finally "threw my heart over" the fence (after a more determined approach) and he followed.

(The lesson here, for those preparing for their first clinic, is to have their horses toughened up for the longer periods of work. Don't worry about yourself, you'll be too apprehensive to get tired.)

After the clinic was over, I had time to ask our still fresh-as-the-proverbial-daisy instructor his overall impressions of North American riders, as compared to their European counterparts.

"North American riders, as a whole, ride very well. They are well-schooled and more stylish than most European jumper riders because of the equitation classes in American shows. When it comes to dressage, Canada (in 1973) is far ahead of the United States. American dressage riders seem to change instructors too often. There are too many differing opinions, which confuse more than they help. I would like to see the best American dressage riders work under one coach and stick with him for at least four years, to give more uniformity to the American dressage style. In comparison, Christillot Hanson Boylen has stuck to one trainer, Willie Schultheiss, for a long time and look how successful she has become!

"One of the main problems, as I see it, is that the science of dressage is not compatible with the American way of life. In business, in car-owning, in home-owning it's change, change, change every few years. To work a horse four years for an Olympic Grand Prix dressage event is not the American style. One is not so quickly in the limelight in dressage.

"Still, dressage can be as popular here as it is in Europe. Like any art form, the beauty of the harmony will prove interesting to the public. Perhaps it will match the rich rewards and the deep satisfaction the rider will experience."

But all's well that ends well as Stability and I take the last fence of the clinic in good style—for us!

As for clinics, Renz believes they can be valuable if repeated every few months. The student and his regular instructor, working constantly together, can get "stale." The good professional welcomes the guest instructor for a little longer, more concentrated work. The students, benefitting from the "new face," seem to listen a little more closely. The new ideas give them "food for thought."

I agreed heartily with Hans Renz. I had learned a lot, and so had my horse. In many ways, the work we had accomplished was the best riding I ever had done.

12 Riding with Rodney Jenkins

Rodney Jenkins stands alone as a rider and trainer of champion hunters and jumpers. Riding such famous show ring stars as Idle Dice, Number One Spy, San Felipe, Gustavus, Not Always, Nanticoke, and Quiet Flight, he has won more blue ribbons, more American Horse Shows Association seasonal championshps, and more prize money than any other rider in history.

Unlike most of today's professional horsemen, however, Jenkins does not do any teaching. The Hilltop Stables show string never has included junior riders nor more than one amateur-owner. Jenkins has been outspoken in stating his aversion to instructing others.

But what if riders did get the chance to ride under the remarkable redhead's supervision? Would his reputation make them more nervous than they would be if riding for another instructor? Would they expect him to teach in an unusual manner? Would his temper match his flaming red hair if they made simple mistakes? Would the master of the timed jump-off admire riders who rode courses at a high rate of speed? Would the outspoken critic of equitation drills praise riders who adopted the "rough and ready" approach?

One group of Eastern riders had the unusual opportunity of being instructed by Rodney Jenkins when the first professional ever named to represent his country in international competition conducted a weekend clinic at Hurdle Hill Farm in the winter of 1977.

What brought this situation about? Jenkins was asked. "I do this only for my friends," the slender rider-trainer stated. "John Shaffner is a good friend of mine and that's the only reason I

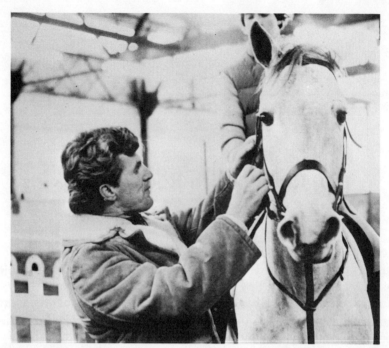

Rodney Jenkins makes a tack adjustment for a young rider during one of his rare clinic appearances, this one at Hurdle Hill Farm in 1977.

agreed to do the clinic. I really don't like to do them and I try to do as few as possible. Winter is vacation time for me. I prefer to stay at home in Virginia and make green horses. Why travel when you don't have to, especially when you travel so much the rest of the year?"

But Jenkins did agree to do the clinic and interest was high among all horsemen in the area. In addition to the forty riders who had signed up for the instruction, the clinic brought out another 150 or so spectators—in bitter cold weather and through dangerous driving conditions—to listen to Jenkins's every word.

Jenkins was equipped with a microphone that could be heard in Hurdle Hill's carpeted, heated lounge, where most of the spectators preferred to sit. And although there was the usual polite chatter in the background during most of the two-day clinic, you could have heard the proverbial "pin" drop when Jenkins twice climbed into the saddle to demonstrate his riding skill. The second time about half the spectators left the lounge to observe from a closer vantage point to the eighty-by-two-hundred-foot arena.

Cynthia Perez, an amateur-owner competitor with her good gray Perfect Stranger, admitted to being "terribly nervous" prior to the clinic, explaining: "I'm going out there with the idea I don't want to make a fool out of myself in front of 'the' Rodney Jenkins. But I also look upon it as a real privilege that not many people have, one to take advantage of. My horse is a bit of a stopper and I have to work on sitting back and holding onto his mouth to keep contact, not dropping contact.

"With a well-known horse it's hard to live up to his past. Stranger had been ridden by Jane Womble and Buddy Brown. When you get a new horse that's won before, everyone rushes to the ring—for perhaps the first year you own him—to see 'What's this fool going to do to the horse this time?' Or that's what you think everyone's thinking. So I feel sorry for another rider, whose horse, Market Rise, had been shown by Rodney on the circuit for a couple of years. I'm more nervous for her than I am for myself."

Joanne Serafini, then fifteen, who had been showing on the "A" circuit for two years, had another approach, feeling, "I wasn't worried because I figured he must have wanted to do the clinic or he wouldn't have come here. Yet I didn't want him to get mad at me." Jayne Schutt, another amateur-owner, thought "He's had so much experience riding green horses that I thought he could do more for me—riding a quite green horse, One For The Road—than any other trainer. He rode my horse, Keelo's Kin, for part of the '76 season, but he hadn't seen me ride since about midyear. John Shaffner, seeing me ride every day and doing the same things, might not always 'see' me completely, not notice those little things that someone else would."

Mrs. Virginia Toksu, an older amateur rider, wondered whether Jenkins "might be such a good rider that he might not make his points understood to an 'average' rider, or be sympathetic to those with less show experience who might be making foolish mistakes, instead of 'thoughtful' mistakes."

Vivian Mittlesteadt, riding a very green Hollydot, declared, "It doesn't bother me to be taught by a superstar. He'll only be here a couple of days and then I'll never have to face him again. John Shaffner and Barbara Bancroft, my regular instructors, are around me all year long—I worry more about what they say about me. On the other hand, Rodney Jenkins has ridden so many horses he probably can get right into you and your problems. I think it'll be interesting to see how he handles us, since he's mainly a rider, not a teacher."

A more familiar sight: Rodney Jenkins competing in an open jumper class aboard Icy Paws. *Photo by Sue Maynard.*

Cynthia "Cynnie" Hunt, an amateur-owner with several years of top show experience, had an advantage: "I've heard him at other clinics, so it won't be an entirely new experience. He's a superior horseman and with his knowledge it should be an excellent clinic and very beneficial. It's a privilege, I feel, to get him to come to Hurdle Hill Farm when he's so busy."

Leslee Clement, then sixteen, was riding the top hunter Columbia, which she had owned less than a month, and "I was scared because I was riding a new horse, not because of the instructor. If I do things wrong I tend to get discouraged fast, and I was hoping I'd do all right. Columbia is so much bigger and longer-striding than my old horse that it took a lot to get adjusted to him." Her brother, Jay, then twelve, felt the clinic would be "really great, getting to ride under a great rider like him, but I'm not really worried."

Tom Brewer, then fourteen, who had been riding for seven years prior to the clinic, felt, "He probably will teach me things differently from the other clinic instructors we've had (Michael

Page, Otis Brown Jr., and Jimmy Williams), or teach them in a different way. My horse, Popsicle, is not green but not 'made.' He's still smarter than I am."

It didn't take much time for both riders and spectators to learn some things about their guest instructor. He was almost unbelievably quick to spot a mistake, or to analyze a horse's or rider's problem. And he made his points with colorful language that was not straight out of the equitation textbooks. He wanted to see a rider who was thinking in advance, who was riding a line of fences with a definite plan. And while he might embarrass a rider with a caustic comment for riding poorly, he always was able to find something in the rider's work to praise later on.

"Don't ever come toward a fence on the wrong lead when I'm teaching you," he told one rider. "Don't sit there dead, do something," he urged another. "Don't let a horse cross-canter before me, that's the worst fault in the world," he warned another rider, adding: "But if you're showing and have to continue the round, then go ahead."

"You are B-L-I-N-D," he stated to another rider. "You keep

"Don't just sit there dead. . . . Do something!" Jenkins exasperatedly told one clinic rider.

riding your mare at a slow 'lick' [pace] and asking her to jump from a long distance. You'll knock the courage and heart out of her. Either ask her to speed up or don't."

"You're running him through like a wild man," he admonished another, continuing: "You think speed carries you places, like a roadrunner. But you have to learn to be patient."

Said one spectator, "He picks up the little, commonsense things you already should know. If you stop and think, what he says is so logical someone really shouldn't have to point it out to you."

Jenkins started off his sessions by asking riders to perform the counter-canter, telling them: "Don't look down. You're circling to the left and we want the left lead so we want to use left rein and leg. When you go into the corner of the ring, hold your left leg against the horse, and hold his head to the inside [of the arena]. Don't bounce off [into the gait], don't move out until you're in complete control. Don't shift your weight on the corner, keep it on the right side of the saddle and use your left leg. Don't let your horse drop onto the forehand, keep him balanced. You can't go into an equitation class if you can't do this, so practice it."

Jenkins then had the riders, one at a time, jog over a little cross rail, pull their mounts up in a straight line, turn around, and do it again. "The object of trotting is to get the horse to the base of the fence and make him use his back," Jenkins told his pupils. "It'll make them quieter, too." Then he had them go through a three-obstacle combination, set low, and then around a course of fences.

Jenkins, however, is a perfectionist. He wanted to see the horse properly on the bit and at the proper rate of speed over the first fence, or he wouldn't let the rider continue. Only about one of every six riders was allowed to continue past the first fence on his first attempt.

Jenkins showed an almost uncanny recall in picking up little hints at what a horse might do later simply by watching—and it didn't look like he was paying particular attention—the riders warm up their horses prior to the start of each clinic session. This was shown when a horse that had been performing excellently over the first part of the course suddenly refused and unseated his rider.

"He was spooking there when you were hacking," Jenkins told the rider. "Now sit back, keep behind him. There [after a successful jump], you learned by your mistake. That's great. When

164

One of the most famous combinations in horse show history, Rodney Jenkins and Idle Dice, competing at the Southampton Show. *Photo by Sue Maynard.*

a horse gets spooking, don't get ducking and pushing. Gather him more, use more leg. He will feel your confidence and he will get confident. When you ride him away from his friends [the other horses in the group], you have to drive a little. bit. When he's coming back to them, you don't."

Here's what Rodney Jenkins had to say about some of the other performances; perhaps you or your own horse commit some of these mistakes, and can benefit from his comments.

"You're a nonchalant rider on the flat and you're nonchalant over a fence. You are letting him crawl along like a mud turtle. You've got to be definite. He's a little lazy and you have to let him know what to do. But let him know it earlier, with a steady pace, instead of trying to do it all in the last two strides."

"You're running him through like a wild man. You knocked the heart out of him over there, asked him too far away from the fence, pushing your hands up his neck. Get your shoulders back, sit still. Nice and quiet. You've got to learn to believe in me."

"You don't need to put a lot of leg on this horse [which Jenkins had often shown for his former owner]. This horse loves

Janice Clement, mounted on Spinnaker, gives noted trainer Rodney Jenkins her undivided attention as he makes a point during a clinic session.

to use his head and neck. Follow through, don't straighten up in the air too soon. If you have two refusals, I don't expect you to wait for me to tell you to punish him with your stick. He wants to play, so we'll make him trot small circles, to both the right and left, in front of the fence. You're not letting him have his way that way, and you're not being mean to him."

"When he looks at something, you back off and drop your hands. That's when you need your contact. Don't drop him, don't get timid when he looks, get aggressive."

"You're pounding his mouth too much. Follow through when you're over a jump. He's not a stopper, so if he gets too strong before a fence you can pull him up and make him back up. I could tell from the way you were making circles you were afraid he'd stop. Be kind coming home [to the other horses], but don't let him get away with spooking and shying."

After seeing another horse jump the cross rail once, Jenkins asked, "He has a tendency to bull [get strong] a little with you, doesn't he?" Jenkins emphasized collecting the horse on the turns

166

and getting him at the proper rate of speed to jump, rather than making the adjustments once the horse had straightened out and was on the approach to a fence.

"Awful. You got desperate. You can't stand prosperity. You start beautifully on your turns and then start speeding up. He has a problem bending to the left." Jenkins laid a pole at the right side of each element of the three-jump combination to help the horse bend his shoulders to the left.

"You have a motor on this horse [which he had shown]. You don't have to 'ride' him. You don't have to get in and make him go, just meet the jump off the turn good. He's got a 'motor' that'll carry him."

"Try to be a little softer with your hands on the circle [before the approach]. He has a tendency to drag to the left, so put your right rein on his neck. Don't straighten up so quick over the fences, that only makes him quicker. 'Soft' doesn't mean hold-on, 'soft' means when he has a nice cadence, leave him alone. You've got to get off his back on the turns. Jumping is no problem with him."

Perhaps Jenkins's most enjoyable moments were watching Market Rise perform with her new rider, Kris Eberlein. He had the

Rodney Jenkins showing Super Flash, a green hunter, at the Lake Placid Show in 1977. The pair won the Hunter Special that year. *Photo by Sue Maynard.*

167

big gray mare just trot into the no-stride, one-stride combination, telling Kris, "Don't put a lot of leg on her. Height means nothing to her. Don't speed up. She can jump any height in the world." And then, after a smoothly performed circuit of the course, Jenkins, with pride in his voice, stated, "That's the way they're supposed to jump, ladies and gentlemen!"

Jenkins later gave a schooling demonstration on Sue Cox's Stash The Cash, a big bay mare who was to compete in the Florida "Sunshine Circuit" in the preliminary jumper division ridden by Debbie Shaffner, John's wife. Here were his comments, made as he rode:

"She's pulling on her front end, so I drop her head, then pick her up, pull a little to the inside and wiggle my rein to the inside to get her to throw her weight to the outside. I keep my weight out of the saddle until I'm ready to pull the horse up, or to bend her.

"Schooling isn't like showing, when you have to take chances and make things look like nothing unusual happened. When you school and they start leaning on the bit, as this mare is doing, you pull them up." As the mare softened and jumped a course set at hunter height, Jenkins added, "I shift my weight in the air over a fence to anticipate turns, but I don't recommend it for amateurs or juniors. It comes with lots of mileage."

Then the fences were raised to the four-foot level and Jenkins gave a beautiful display of riding skills, commenting: "This mare has a super hind end. I have to support her front end, have to grab her a bit before a fence, but I always follow through in the air. As she gets more confidence in me, she's trusting me, she's waiting— and I'm out of breath.

"I put my leg forward and my seat back so I can control and drive better. [After a short turn] I was meeting it wrong and I didn't increase speed, just waited. Speed just adds to your problems. She's jumped cleaner but she's backing up more on the approach. I trust my eye. I saw I was close, so I didn't 'nick' her. Your eye can't cost you anything—but your life."

After the clinic, Jenkins's students were unanimous in their praise of the great horseman and how much they had learned from him.

Said Mrs. Toksu: "I was surprised at his patience, his thoughtfulness. He tried to put you at your ease and make everything seem comfortable and logical. He rode my horse after she stopped

Rodney Jenkins and the great Idle Dice clearing a triple bar en route to victory in the Cleveland Grand Prix in the Chagrin Falls Show in 1977. This win and one at the Ox Ridge Show, plus consistent placings, gave "RJ" and "Ike" enough points to win the "Grand Prix Horse of the Year" title. *Photo by Sue Maynard.*

a couple of times, schooled her, and then said 'I think it's you, not her.' But she's green and needed an aggressive rider. Rather than just picking up things about your horse, he picked out things about you, to give you something to work on afterwards. You can't teach 'feel,' but he shows you what to do to work toward it. It's all so logical, once he tells you. You get to the point where you jump a bad fence and adjust for it the next time instead of just going along. 'You're a pretty rider but not an aggressive one,' he told me."

"He's not just a brilliant teacher, he's a genius," said Vivian Mittlesteadt. "He can tell you on every stride what you're doing wrong, and get it across to you. He was critical but I didn't mind that, it was a fantastic experience. Sometimes you'd wish you'd make a mistake, so you might learn more. I had such a cold that if it was anyone else I wouldn't have ridden the second day. My

Rodney Jenkins and Idle Dice, winners of the 1977 Cleveland Grand Prix, waiting for the victory gallop with runner-up Bernie Traurig and The Cardinal. *Photo by Sue Maynard.*

horse went the best he had ever gone. I had listened, so I went nice and slow setting him up in the corners, sitting and waiting for my fences, and getting to my spots before the fences much better. I was in the beginners group and I told him 'I'll see you next time,' and he told me 'I expect to see you in a higher group.' "

Joanne Serafini remembered, "He said I had to get with my horse better. I let him get too heavy on the forehand. He had me circle to get his mind off rushing, to get him collected and together. He also had me work on getting him to land on the proper lead over a fence. He's a perfectionist. If you didn't do it right he made you keep repeating it 'til you did."

"I liked the individual attention he gave," said Cindi Perez. "He didn't 'ice' things over. He laid it on the line. I heard everything from 'You rode that line very well' to the other extreme, 'That fence was absolutely terrible.' "

"I liked him a lot," said Tom Brewer. "He made it easy to learn. He worked on my turns. I wasn't bending my horse enough and

170

getting deep enough into the corners. I wasn't using my inside leg enough and I wasn't using my indirect rein behind the withers. Before, my horse was bending his head to the outside while turning. He wants you to keep it bent to the inside. I also have a bad habit of not keeping my head up. He got to 'bugging' me about it and I think it's improved, a little."

"Yes, that was me on the wrong lead on the counter-canter," admitted Leslee Clement. "Rodney Jenkins was much stricter than I thought he'd be, but he had seen my horse perform and he could give me a lot of clues."

"With my horse it was no big problem, other than 'mileage,' more experience," said Jayne Schutt. "We worked on getting soft and quiet, and did lots of circles. But he didn't let me stop on the approach because my horse would have gotten mad instead of quiet."

"I was frozen stiff, but really impressed with the way he expressed himself," said Jay Clement. "He helped quiet my horse a lot. He helped me to get my changes of lead better by setting my

Rodney Jenkins (far left), Bernie Traurig, Michael Hunter, and Kathy Kusner (in windbreaker) at the takeoff for the water jump in the Adirondack Grand Prix at the Lake Placid Show in 1977. *Photo by Sue Maynard.*

171

horse on his hocks. He tried to make your horse go to the first fence in a nice frame and leave from a nice spot, looking pretty—instead of just going."

"I thought it was an excellent clinic," said Cynnie Hunt. "His criticism was very constructive, very beneficial. He doesn't concentrate on any one thing but takes an overview. I was riding a young Quarter Horse field hunter who hadn't done much ring work. He came forward through the triple combination, a type of fence he wasn't used to. We got him to good spots to keep his willing jumping attitude. He has a high head carriage, so Rodney put a pole down on each side of the cross rail to get him to look down, and lower his head. I won't be riding this horse that much in the coming showing year, but I still gained knowledge of how to work on horses with similar problems.

"Rodney Jenkins explains his exercises and why they'll help. You can't have any doubt in your mind about what he says to do. I've seen him do it, and it works."

Despite the appreciation and enthusiasm of his students, Jenkins does not plan to change his methods of operation in the foreseeable future. "I now have the patience to work with youngsters," he said, "but right now do not have the time. Riding twenty or so horses doesn't permit it. I've tried it, but the youngsters wind up being coached by others in our stable and it just isn't fair to them.

"I would like to train two or three youngsters, to bring them along to do some of the riding for me when I decide to slow down. But it doesn't look like I'll be doing either—training juniors or slowing down—for a while. One of the problems is that I can see them trot around the ring once or twice and can tell which have outstanding talent. I think it would be too boring working with those without unusual talent. I like excitement in my life, and right now training juniors and amateurs doesn't seem exciting enough for me."

13 Common Mistakes
Seen in the Show Ring

If every horse and rider in every horse show class performed perfectly, horse shows would run for twenty hours each day. But rarely do either horses or riders, especially beginners, perform as well as they are capable of doing. Many times it's "show nerves" and excitement that throw them off. Frequently, though, it's so fundamental an error by the rider that he could virtually crawl away and hide from embarrassment once he realizes his mistake.

There are obvious miscalculations that remove all chance of a winning performance even before horse and rider arrive at the show. These include the lack of proper training and grooming that immediately attract the attention of spectators and show officials —in a negative manner. Another is not arriving early enough to make your entries properly and school your horse in the show ring or over the hunt course.

The more you participate in shows the more mistakes you probably will make; hopefully you will learn from them and not repeat them. But there do seem to be certain show ring errors that are common to all riders, and this chapter will discuss some of them.

The main thing I see, as I'm announcing small, local shows, is what seems to be a complete mental fog envelop many riders, especially in a walk-trot-canter or other pleasure-type class. After watching only a few such classes, anyone can tell that the routine is going to be walk, jog/trot, lope/canter, reverse, and the same three gaits in the same order once again. Yet rider after rider finishes the trot portion of the class, gets himself stuck in the

It doesn't have to happen in a big indoor show, it can happen anywhere—and frequently does. Falls are part of riding. *Photo by Sue Maynard.*

midst of a group of horses, and then has all sorts of trouble getting his mount into a good position from which to strike off into the canter.

Instead, the thinking rider should finish the trot and then come to a halt, if necessary, to get some room in front of and behind his mount. Then he can give the horse the canter signals without worrying about another careening past and unsettling him.

It doesn't require an advanced degree in showmanship to notice a horse that appears to be too much for his rider and to try to keep at least half a ring's distance from that pair. The same for a horse that seems inclined to kick or bite. Don't let your horse get near such rogues. Horses like to imitate each other. Pick the oldest and most settled horse and the most experienced rider to follow around the ring. Not only may your horse imitate the "old pro" in his manners, but the judge's glance also may pass from the expert rider onto show newcomer you—and stay there a little longer.

A show and its various distractions are bound to make your horse more on edge than normal. You must get to the show early to work him until he settles down. If he's simply too much for you to handle, try to get a more experienced rider to work him for you, or ride him in an early class. If your horse can jump perhaps it would be best to have an expert rider take him into a hunter class even if you only plan to show him in nonjumping classes. The work over jumps should settle him down. Many wise jumper riders enter their horses in an early hunter class just to use it as a "school" for the later competition over higher fences.

In general, a horse needs less emphatic aids in a show than he might need at home. I found this out to my regret in the first show I ever entered riding one of John Shaffner's horses, The Plainsman. He had a slight problem with one canter lead. I was so bound and determined that he was going to get it right that I pushed so strongly I pushed the poor horse into a cross canter. Hesitating a second to allow a nearby horse to lead Plainsman into the canter and light aids probably would have done the trick.

You have to be a bit of an actor to be a successful show rider. You have to put on a "poker face" and not help the judge to "see" any mistakes he might have missed. If your horse gives a little buck or kick while cantering in a hunter under-saddle class,

John Shaffner talks things over with Beth Snyder, riding Breathtaking, prior to a class at the Chagrin Falls Horse Show. *Photo by Sue Maynard.*

for instance, don't get a cross look on your face and start yanking and pulling. Sit quietly, keep a pleasant expression—maybe he didn't notice it.

I never like to see a beginning rider in a class over fences enter the ring without carrying a crop (if you can't manage the reins and a crop perhaps you don't belong in the ring), because nothing looks more stupid, nor so ineffective as seeing a rider on a horse that has refused to jump a fence sitting there slapping the horse with his hand or his hunt cap. Use the crop behind the leg, never in front of the girth.

If the horse refuses, make him stop squarely in front of the fence and take a good look at it. Then turn around promptly, make as small a circle as you can and still have a proper approach, and try again. Backing the horse before making the circle of approach can help get the horse's hocks under him and give him more impulsion for his second try. Don't, don't, don't trot "ten miles" away from the fence and then rush, rush, rush on your approach. The longer distance and the greater speed can only excite the horse more, or give him more time to fix the idea of refusing more firmly into his mind.

A junior exhibitor keeping an eye on judge Jim Becker while keeping her cropout Paint properly posed in a showmanship class. *Courtesy t. h. e. Studio; photo by Ken Schmidt.*

As the show goes on and the excitement of the first class or two wears off, your horse and yourself may need some waking up instead of some calming down. Maybe he needs a slap on the rump with your crop before he goes into the ring. Instead of boring circles at the trot in the warm-up area he might need something more challenging: trot and stop, canter or lope from a halt, five to seven steps backwards, and the like. Have him alert and responsive. Keep the warm-up session short. Retain some "ring magic" for the rest of your classes.

First impressions in the ring very often are the best, or longest-lasting. If you know the course for a hunter class, for instance, it often helps to be the first rider in the class. Going first shows the judge you have studied the course diagram and you are mentally ready. If you have a good trip it sets a standard that the others have to surpass.

It is the judge and the ringmaster whose directions you must follow. The announcer is only their echo. You obey his voice, of course, but he may not always be correct. I once caused a rider to miss a ribbon in a show I was announcing. I looked up, saw the rider clear a fence that was the last fence in the previous class, and said "Thank you, Number 425." The only problem was that the fence now was the third from the last fence in the new class. The

In a huge halter class such as this it is impossible to keep a horse posed properly from its start to its finish. *Courtesy AQHA.*

rider wasn't sure enough in her own mind and promptly pulled up her horse upon hearing my announcement. Don't depend on the announcer, depend on yourself!

Sometimes a show prize list is printed wrong and does not conform to the rules. I once was a steward at an Arabian show where the judge worked from the printed program and in a park horse class simply asked for a "trot." A rider in the ring asked me, as she trotted past, "What kind of a trot does he want?" A quick glance through the A.H.S.A. rule book indicated that the proper gait was a "park trot," one with brilliance. This rider was prepared for the class, the judge and I were not.

Before you get the idea that I always seem to be around whenever an error is being committed, I ought to claim those are the only mistakes I've ever made as either an announcer or steward. I might even be correct. Those are the only mistakes I remember making—recently. But now might be a good time to abandon the author's prerogative to be first and mention mistakes observed by professional horsemen who have been in a lot more show rings than I have.

Barbara Cratty and her husband, John, have trained and shown fourteen national champion Quarter Horses in the last few years. They are best known for their campaigning of the great Pecho Dexter, who accumulated more points for wins in English and Western pleasure and at halter than any other horse in the Quarter Horse breed's history. Mrs. Cratty believes too many young show riders "ride blind." The attractive, blond horsewoman, whose home stable is in Marion, Ohio, explained it this way:

"The youngsters simply aren't ringwise; they do not know where they are going. When the show announcer asks them to lope, they jump right into it, regardless of whether or not the horse in front of them is loping or trotting or walking or even momentarily checked and standing. They think the announcer's words are a life or death matter, so if he says 'trot,' then trot they must, regardless of what anyone else is doing. When that happens and it affects a horse I'm riding, or a horse one of my pupils is riding, it really aggravates me."

Mrs. Cratty also sees many new showmen who have nice horses but don't know how to present them properly to the judge, especially in a halter class.

"John was judging a really big show in Houston one fall," she recalled. "You'd think a youngster entered in a show like that

Mike and Cheryl Leppard, Canadian professionals, shown here with Gay Magnolia, believe too many new show ring competitors spend more time "knocking" professionals than trying to learn from them.

would be fairly ring-wise. But I noticed one young fellow who was standing near the head of the line in a halter or youth activity showmanship class (I can't remember which).

"Well, someone must have really emphasized to him that he must show his horse every minute of the class. He had that horse posed right when my husband was looking him over and he kept the horse posed right all the time John was going down the line. But by the time John came back to look a second time, the boy's poor horse was just worn out; he simply fell to pieces. There were 110 horses in the class. Now, if the boy had just given the horse a little breather, a little rest some time during the class, he'd have been ready to pose again when it really counted.

"Too many exhibitors in halter classes either pay too much attention to the horse, as this boy did, or too much attention to the judge and not enough to the horse.

"An animal is an animal, and he can give you his attention only

A properly attired Western rider ready for the show ring. The look is neat and workmanlike for both Heather Howell and Worth's Drifter.

so long. This halter class I'm talking about took an hour to judge. This boy showed his horse for the entire hour—to nobody! You have to know your horse and know how long he can look lively and interested in what's going on and keep that pose. When he's near the end of his rope, so to speak, you have to let him move a little and relax.

"In the youth activity showmanship class you and I just saw, my pupil, Karen Moody, who is only fourteen and began showing seriously only this year, didn't know where she was going. She let her mare, Miss Okie Bailey, get next to a mare that was acting sour. I told her before the class to stay away from that mare but she didn't listen. So her mare was distracted while she was showing it to the judge, and she lost a good ribbon." (The judge backed up Mrs. Cratty's observations, taking time to tell Karen why he was placing her only fifth.) "She'll probably listen to me a little more carefully from now on," Barbara added.

Mrs. Cratty sees lots of mothers and fathers doing the grooming

180

while their sons or daughters get ready for halter showing classes, but believes this procedure must change when a child is showing extensively.

"When I'm hauling a child and a horse for national honors," she said, "I'm driving five to ten hours at a stretch. The child is sleeping all that time. Now I'm just not able to be up bright and early the next day to groom her horse as well as the one or two I might be showing, which helps to keep the travel costs down for the youngster's parents. I'll help them, of course, but they have to learn how to do it all—take care of their horse's stall, feed him, groom him, blanket him, bandage him, and all the rest. There are a lot of miles to be traveled if you're going to accumulate those championship points, and the youngster has to assume his or her share of the work.

"One other thing a youngster has to learn to do to be a successful showman is to listen to the trainer—both before and during the class. She has to be alert to catch a hint as she comes by the rail where you're standing, when you tell her to change what she's been doing.

"Yes, I know we trainers and parents aren't supposed to be coaching from the sidelines, but everyone does it!" Mrs. Cratty added with a laugh.

Tommy and Sue Ryan have shown such top Quarter Horses as supreme champion Diamond Duro; Man O Glow, who was nearing his supreme rating when the Ryans were interviewed; two-time Western pleasure champion Carmel and reining horse Smoked Out. They believe clothing and equipment too often are overlooked by people just beginning to compete in shows.

"It's not the cost," Tommy emphasizes. "You don't have to have the most expensive clothing in the ring. But it must be up to date and it must fit you properly and it must be neat. One of the biggest mistakes is wearing pants that are too short. You have to realize that pants that fit just right when you are standing are going to be too short when you are up on your horse."

The length the Ryans advise depends on the material of the pants. When I was interviewing them Sue was wearing a pair of brown saddle pants that just about met the ground at her boot heels. But later she was wearing a pair of white pants that had to be rolled up about three inches while she was on the ground.

"Even a $5 hat can be steamed and creased so it looks proper,"

Sue Ryan feels many riders don't allow for the wrinkles that develop in riding pants when the wearer is mounted. These summer-weight slacks must be rolled up three inches while Sue is on the ground.

Tommy continued. "Judges notice these things. A neat-looking hat and proper-length pants make you look like you know what you are doing. Another thing that is going to count against an exhibitor is his own grooming, especially the boys. Perhaps these 'cowboy judges' from the West are more conservative types than us Easterners, but they definitely want to see neatly cut hair on a boy."

The Ryans have seen youngsters go into halter or showmanship classes with rope halters and shanks—a sure sign of someone who is inexperienced in showing. It doesn't have to be a silver-mounted halter, as the top professionals use, but it should be leather and it should be clean and in good condition.

Another mistake many newcomers to showing make is not preparing sufficiently in advance, especially for halter classes. Many of these exhibitors appear never to have even tried to stand their horses properly prior to entering the ring.

When it comes to horsemanship, Sue Ryan believes too many young riders do not know how to use their hands properly. "They just don't know what a 'feel' of the horse's mouth means," she explains. "If you tell them to loosen up with their hands, they lose their balance in the saddle. This is because they do not have a secure seat to begin with, and also because their horses are not collected under them. If he is collected you can feel his mouth much more easily."

Sue thinks many youngsters are riding and showing today merely because many of their friends are riding. They do not really work at riding or horsemanship and will never take the time to prepare themselves properly for shows. And many of them are riding simply because their parents want them to.

Paul Oswald, a Canadian horseman who has campaigned such top horses as King Clipper Joe and Show Tip, believes there is too much emphasis on winning today. Bigger shows lead to higher-priced horses and less of the "good-time, friendly" spirit that marked shows of a few years ago.

But when Sue Ryan is mounted on Sondra Bixler, the pants are rolled down and hit her boots just right.

"Everyone used to have a good time together after a show," he said. "Now, as soon as one show is over everyone packs up to go home or go to the next show. It's simply not a hobby any more. As a result, too many horses are overtrained and overridden in an effort to win trophies, blue ribbons, and American Quarter Horse Association points. People are not taking the time necessary to properly train a horse and produce him for the show ring. They are asking the horse for more than he can give at his age or stage of training.

"In reining classes, which I have shown in more often than other classes, the riders try to make every run a super one. They are making the horses stop too hard, and sit down hard and slide. When it comes to the roll-back after the stop, they are not letting the horse run down, sit down and then come around. They are trying for these real wild roll-backs, trying to make the horse jump around the other way.

"And along with this, it is obvious the horses are being made to run the pattern too often at home, and work too often in a ring."

Mike Leppard, of Ottawa, Ontario, has shown two horses—Sugar Joe Reed and Salty Red Rose—who became AQHA champions in thirteen and fourteen shows, respectively. He also handled Gay Magnolia, a full sister to 1972 halter champion Magnolia Gay.

"Too many amateur exhibitors spend all their time knocking the professionals instead of trying to learn from us," said Mike. "We *should* be doing more winning than the amateurs—it's our full-time business. But nearly any trainer will be glad to give an amateur some pointers if he's approached in the proper manner and at the proper time—when he isn't busy at a show. After all, if we're nice to you, perhaps you'll remember us when you're looking for your next horse or when you decide to campaign extensively.

"The main thing beginners do is ride their horses too much both at home and before a class, and get them ring sour. It's the same thing with feeding. More horses are overfed and overworked than underfed and underworked.

"If you are hauling horses for national championships they do not need a lot of work. They keep in shape simply by being on their feet in a trailer and bumped and jounced around as they go down the road.

"Proper clothing—up to date, well fitting, and neat—is very important. Judges like a neat appearance, and seem to discriminate against boys with long hair. It may not be right, but they seem to do it. In a halter class you have to have your horse groomed to perfection and properly trimmed, especially his face and bridle path behind his ears.

"To present a horse well you can't overshow him. You can't keep working at the horse and forget where the judge is. You can't keep 'picking' at your horse constantly in the ring. You have to give him a chance to relax from time to time. And a halter horse must be kept out of the sun if you want his coat to look its best.

"When you campaign on both sides of the border, as I do, you have to be sure the proper forms and certificates are up to date and correctly filled in by a veterinarian. These forms also are required in many individual states, so American riders need to be aware of them also.

"When you spend a lot of time on the road, you have to take pains to keep your horses eating properly. I try to take our own feed from home with me as much as possible. I also find that horses seem to like country water, without chlorine, much better than city water."

In the show ring, it takes only one nervous, disorganized amateur to foul up a ring filled with professionals, Leppard contends. "They think they are the only ones in the ring and they go around bouncing off other horses and the rail or walls of rings or indoor arenas. They watch their own horse and no one else's."

John Shaffner believes lack of concentration is the biggest problem beginning show riders have, whether they are children or adults.

"You can have a 'green' [inexperienced] rider repeat back to you some last-minute instructions," he declared, "and then they'll go right into a ring and forget everything. You are lucky if they can even remember the order of fences they are going to jump.

"This pressure usually starts building as soon as they get to the show. They're excited and nervous, they want to talk to their friends, they worry about the different fences and the difference in the show ring. Then they want to school really well—there is just too much on their minds.

"Adults are subject to the same pressures—if they haven't shown as children—and are probably more self-conscious because

"An inexperienced rider can repeat your instructions right back to you, then go into the ring and forget everything," according to John Shaffner. *Photo by Sue Maynard.*

of their ages. In addition, they have the nagging thought 'Who'll cook the meals if I fall off and get hurt?'

"There is only one way to correct this problem and that is 'mileage': the more you ride and perfect your form, the less you have to concentrate on when you're in the ring. The more shows you go to the less you think about all the distractions and the more you can concentrate on riding well and showing your horse.

"In an equitation class, many young riders are simply too loose in the saddle. Sometimes this is tension. Instead of getting really deep into the saddle and sitting 'into' the horse, the riders tighten up their muscles—thinking they're strengthening their grip—but instead they are squeezing themselves up further on top of the horse, almost into a ball. The more you are 'into' the horse the more you can feel what he is doing, or about to do.

"Many beginning riders in an equitation class over fences eliminate themselves as soon as they go into a ring. Some make a sloppy, irregular circle on their approach to the first fence—and some don't even circle, just rush at the fence. This, again, is due to lack of concentration.

"I think the most common fault I see in equitation classes is a lack of use of the legs and too much use of the hands. Judges are looking for a fluid performance with no rough movements. I try to teach young riders how to keep a 'feel' of the horse's mouth from becoming a 'vise'-grip.

"On the other hand, there are youngsters who trust their horses too much. Just because your horse has jumped a fence in the schooling area, or in the first class, doesn't mean he will do it every time. You can't simply drop your hands down on his neck two or three strides from a fence and 'trust' him to get over. You have to support him with your legs and hands right into the takeoff point. Once a horse is in the air, you could cut the reins right off the bridle—but you'll never get in the air if the horse doesn't leave the ground.

"When a horse refuses a fence, many inexperienced riders take him back fifty to one hundred feet and run him back to it. Speed doesn't make a horse jump. It would be better, if the fence was three feet or three-and-a-half feet high, to go back about fifteen feet or so, support the horse well with hands and legs, be sure he sees the fence, and ride him over it.

"When riders get more experience they don't make as many basic mistakes but often develop other new, bad habits. Some begin getting too high out of the saddle over fences, or begin ducking their heads to one side over one fence and then maybe to the other side over the next fence. The whole secret of riding in hunter and horsemanship classes is to try to make every fence 'ride' the same way.

"Many riders, over a course of three-and-a-half-foot fences, ask a horse to stand back too far from the jump instead of riding him to within three-and-a-half feet from the fence, which will make a more natural, fluid jump. These riders have not yet developed an eye for distance, they don't know how to steady their horses between fences. They do know if they ride their horse strongly into the fence that he'll jump it—they hope.

"They don't think eight 'nice' fences, they think it's better to stand back and try for eight 'big' fences. Again, this is lack of concentration or experience.

"Years ago, if a rider didn't want to spend the time working on proper riding form for equitation and hunter classes but had a pretty good 'natural seat,' he would enter jumper classes. The courses they were building then were just a bunch of fences that you could ride at and get over and win a ribbon.

"Today the courses are a lot more complicated in jumper classes. There are fences in combination, changes of distances on the different lines of the course—you have to have better control of your horse, so you have to learn to sit quieter, use your aids a lot quicker and smoother, and generally be a more polished rider."

Victor Hugo-Vidal, one of the East's leading trainers and judges, feels too many riders "think about themselves too much and not enough about their horses. They become too involved with style and form, and are too quick to blame the horse. They are overly concerned with how they look on the horse and become rigid. It is the overall trip that counts. Buddy Brown has done a lot for the equitation division because of his lovely feel for the horse. He has a God-given gift to look good over a total trip around a course of fences, although he is not picture perfect at every instant."

If Stephanie Griep, Tom Brewer, and Jennifer Elden remember John Shaffner's instructions, they will avoid many mistakes common to most young riders. *Courtesy t. h. e. Studio; photo by Ken Schmidt.*

Mrs. Gabor Francia-Kiss feels that many young or inexperienced riders make one of two mistakes: "Either they run the horse into or under the fence, getting in too close, or they go 'check' crazy, they check, check, and check the horse with the reins until they are crawling around the course."

Roger Young shudders when he sees "a completely unprofessional approach, an air of frantic disorganization with no planning ahead of how the rider will ride the round.

"Many times you can see the youngsters go completely blank as they make a circle in the ring. They are uptight, overwrought, they don't follow any plan they might have made before they came in the in-gate. The way to correct it, other than the obvious one of just getting them to more shows, is to explain what they did wrong. You don't yell or scream from ringside. You talk to them, you keep your voice normal, like a dinner conversation. Explain in terms they can understand. Joke with them about it to relax them.

"It's almost the same thing with the inexperienced horse. Prevent bad experiences. A green horse will stop if he is in wrong on his approach to a fence. Let him, don't fight him or punish him—unless he's a persistent quitter, then he has to be made to go over the fence. But every horse and every rider is a unique individual, there are no hard and fast rules to apply to mistakes."

Liz Horey, who helped start out many young show riders at upstate New York's smaller shows, sees many mistakes committed by "green" riders of all ages: "New show riders seem to feel 'secure' in the middle of the pack of a group of horses in a hack class, for example. But this is how you can get your horse kicked or yourself covered up. You have to train your eye to look for the open spot, where the judge can see you.

"It may seem strange to mention this, but many riders have trouble riding in their first shows because of their clothing. They are not used to riding in breeches and boots. Those items generally are newly purchased, so they might be a bit tight or stiff. It's a different feeling to go from jeans and schooling chaps and short boots or shoes to breeches and high boots. It's good to have a few lessons or schools at home in your show ring clothes.

"In the ring riders tend to 'freeze up' mentally. They don't think before the fences. They seem to 'lose' their horse around the corners, letting them cut to the inside of the ends of the ring, and letting them get out of balance. Often they forget about lead changes if there is a change of direction in a class over fences. So they come off the end not really in control and miss the first fence of a line. Then, because their composure and poise are not well-developed, they miss the second and third fences on the line, too. A more experienced rider can have a bad fence, then pull himself and his horse together and recover.

"Riders seem to have the most trouble with their hands, resting them down on the horse's neck and letting them get flat on top, with their knuckles parallel to the ground. Then their lower legs get too far in front of them. It is quite hard for a beginner to train himself to get his seat in the front part of the saddle and his legs back underneath him. The lower leg must be active, and many riders have trouble getting their heels down. I try to work with them to 'break the ankle in half,' separating the lower leg from the heel. One way this can be improved is by standing on a stair with the balls of the feet, the heel extending over the edge, and bouncing. Deep-knee bends for five or ten minutes a day also will help.

"When it comes to a hunter or equitation course of jumps, beginning show riders are very stride-conscious, which they should

Sometimes, no matter how well you prepare for a class, things simply go wrong. *Photo by Sue Maynard.*

190

be. But if it's a 'going' seven strides down a line, for example, they tend to override the first fence—which really isn't part of the line. If it's a 'steady' five stride line, on the other hand, they'll 'park' at the first fence: shorten stride so much that the horse is not covering enough ground. You must learn to ride the first fence of a line as an individual fence, then close your leg to go for a long distance or steady your horse for a lesser distance. The rider with more experience learns to open up or steady while going around the corners of the ring. The beginners oversteady or override."

Once riders begin to accumulate a little show ring "mileage" and begin to be aware of where their hands and legs should be and how to coordinate their bodies with the horse's movements, they may begin to expect too much of themselves, Miss Horey believes. "It especially is a problem with those youngsters who have some natural talent," she explains. "They 'fly' through the basics and think all their progress will be that rapid and that easy. But all riders hit a plateau sooner or later, and then it takes more time to improve.

"Certainly younger riders are more agile and supple and have an easier time with their riding at first. Usually they have not developed any bad habits. But I think the beginning amateur owner is the most rewarding pupil to work with. Physically he is not as adaptable as a youngster, but he can comprehend the theory of riding so much easier.

"When it comes to mistakes, the older rider has a greater fear of being hurt and a greater fear of making a mistake and looking foolish. So he will tense up in the ring more than the younger rider. However, there is much more peer group pressure among the junior riders. They are very much aware of how well each other rides, and they are very competitive. The adults are in the show ring to have fun, because it's their hobby. The kids are out there to win!

"This can lead to some nervousness, but the youngsters seem to be able to make a mistake and pull themselves together easier. An adult with the same amount of show ring experience misses one fence, and usually that's the trend for the rest of the class or the day. The youngster seems to be able to start 'fresh' in the next class much more easily."

One of the newer hunter-jumper show divisions, and one that can lead to problems for younger riders, is the "children's hunter" division. The fences are only two and a half feet high and the riders generally are beginners. The division was designed for the hunter pony, the small hunter, or the half-bred hunter—the typical "first show horse." But as shows become more competitive the beginning show rider with the highly experienced "made" show horse is often seen in such classes, even at one-day shows.

Miss Horey points out that "Ponies have to cover more ground, because the courses are designed for horses. So it's generally going to be a more 'going' stride for a pony hunter and the riders are going to tend to override the first fence. Another problem is that the child often forgets that it is the horse that is being judged in children's hunter classes. He can have eight perfect fences but he might not get a ribbon. The quality of jumping is getting better and better, so if his horse is not 'pretty' over his fence the rider is just out of luck. It might be a fine, well-ridden trip, but if the youngster's horse isn't as nice a horse as another that's ridden equally as well. . . .

"What you do in cases like that is tell the rider to do as well as

If your yearling can stand and pose correctly outside the show ring, with its many distractions, then he surely will do as well in actual competition. At least, Bob Harbour hopes so.

he can, and do what you (the instructor) want him to do. That's what counts. Sometimes it will take a different horse or a different division to earn a ribbon. But it's hard for a youngster to understand. They want those ribbons now! That's one reason the numerical judging system is good. If a score improves from a sixty-two to a sixty-five from one class to another he can still feel a sense of accomplishment, even if the lowest score that wins a ribbon is a seventy."

A first horse show can be a long, long day. The rider's excitement often may make him forget just how many hours are slipping by. As in all matters dealing with horsemanship, the horse's comfort and well-being must come first. If you don't have a class for a while, get out of the saddle, loosen the girth, give your horse a drink. If you have a stall to use, put him inside for a bit. If you have a trailer, tie him to it—securely, and from a halter, not his bridle—preferably where he'll have some shade. But check on him every once in a while, don't forget him completely.

Remember that a horse show is a show. You are a performer. Whether there are twenty spectators or two thousand, try to give your best performance for them. Be happy about being in the ring. Look good, feel good, and be proud of yourself and your horse. If you or he makes a mistake at a fence, make your correction and try again promptly. If he just won't go near a trail class obstacle, make a pass or two at it and then forget it and go on to the next.

Every time you get on your horse's back it's schooling—one more brick in the foundation of what will hopefully be a pyramid toward the finished, perfect horse and rider. This especially is true of each experience in the show ring. Let's make them as happy as possible. Train at home, "show" at the show.

14 Judging Complaints: English Style

A popular television comedy show made the phrase "Here comes the judge" almost a household word. But whereas the phrase brought smiles to viewers, a similar phrase applied to a horse show judge usually brings frowns. Horse shows have become more and more popular and probably will continue to grow in direct proportion to the increasing numbers of horse owners. You own your horse, train him, care for him—naturally you think he is beautiful and talented; eventually you want to have your opinion confirmed by a noted horseman/judge.

It's only human nature to rate a judge in terms of how he rated your horsemanship or your horse's performance in the past. This changes as one becomes more educated and experienced. Yet the more one shows or attends shows, the more one seems to hear the same comments being made about English show judges. The persistent rumblings cannot simply be dismissed as the "sour grapes" of losers—even winning owners, trainers, and riders are joining the chorus:

"You see the same judges over and over."

"We need to develop new judges."

"There are too many horsemen who do nothing but judge, they make their living at it."

"The price of horses is so high that judges who deal in horses—and ninty-five per cent of them do—have to 'take care' of those to whom they have sold high-priced horses in the past."

"There is a small clique of show managers and judges who keep each other in the business, and virtually control the major horse shows."

As the price of proven ribbon- and trophy-winners goes up, there

A nonjumping class in an English horse show nears its completion, and the judge, Mrs. Chris Duffield, makes one last check of the riders' numbers.

can be no doubt that there is more pressure on the judge or judges at a major horse show. He is in the middle of the ring with twenty or thirty horses worth $3,000 to $50,000 each. They are well trained, well ridden, beautifully turned out. Many have made outstanding reputations by past performances. Classes are larger and larger. At an "A"-rated show it is common to have more than twenty horses in a class over fences. The Florida shows often have one hundred or more green and novice hunters. Just staying awake and alert for the two or three hours required to judge such a class requires a superhuman effort.

Showing is big business for the professional horseman. Operating a major horse show is just as big, and more complex, an undertaking. Shows have huge expenditures in renting or improving their grounds; maintaining jumps, loudspeakers, and other equipment; renting temporary stalls; hiring judges and other personnel; and providing food and other necessities for the competitors and general public. Without large entries, the show cannot be a success. Without a "name" judge, the largest stables will not send their entries through the booth.

Who are the best hunter/equitation judges? Generally they are the proven professionals with the good "track records" of having judged at the biggest shows without offending anyone with their

195

work or their behavior. Thev don't hold grudges, they don't have drinking problems. The long hours of the show—and the socializing afterwards—do not leave them in a sour frame of mind for the next day.

One of them is Stephen O. Hawkins, who agrees that there should be more judges officiating at the best shows, but also points out the "A" show managers like to stick with those who are reliable, who have no axe to grind with any exhibitor. Their judging means more entries for the show. There has been talk of assigning "guest judges" or "junior judges" to work with the top judges at shows, to learn from them and to have them check their "unofficial" judging. But at the bigger shows there simply isn't time for it. And most of the exhibitors seem to resent the presence of younger horsemen in the ring in any capacity, official or otherwise. He noted:

"There has been talk of having a vote of exhibitors and getting a consensus of the top thirty to fifty judges and having the American Horse Shows Association assign judges 'out of a hat' so to speak. That would be chaos. The rule that judges cannot judge more than one 'A' show per month in an area of two hundred road miles restricts judges quite a bit. I am approached by representatives of more than two hundred shows, and do about thirty-five. Even for one-day shows it is getting more difficult, especially in the East. I have turned down shows, talked to the officials a couple of weeks later, and found they had to call thirty to thirty-five judges before they could find one who wasn't busy on that date or restricted from judging in their areas."

Although the AHSA rule book emphasizes the importance of giving younger judges the opportunity of working with experienced judges, there is no rule that forces shows to do so; many horsemen feel mandating the suggestion would help the situation tremendously.

How does one go about becoming a judge, since nearly everyone agrees there is a need for more of them? First, you obviously must know quite a bit about hunters and hunter seat riding—to name just two of some twenty different divisions of horse show competition. This experience usually comes through competing in such divisions as a rider, owner, or trainer.

Many horsemen feel it is too easy to become a judge. The applicant needs letters of recommendation from six persons, three of whom must be judges or members of AHSA committees. At

196

this point one becomes a "recorded" judge. He may not judge alone in an "A" or "B" show. But after judging only two shows in three years he can be advanced to "recognized" judge, and then can judge alone at an "A" show.

The most important thing, once you accept a job to judge, is to be organized, to have a system of judging a class so that you can quickly separate the horses into "good," "fair," and "poor" and pick your ribbon-winners accordingly. You must have a method by which you can mark down good and bad portions of the performance so that you can refer to them if you are questioned by a rider or trainer after the class is over. As a new judge, it is quite likely that you will be asked to do some explaining at your first few shows. The way you handle yourself initially may determine your eventual success or failure as a horse show judge.

In a hunter class, there are two phases of the performance: galloping and jumping. There is no rule that states which phase is to count for what percentage of the final score. Some judges place more emphasis on "way of going," some on jumping ability. What exhibitors insist upon, however, is consistency. If you prefer a

Many show ring riders believe horse shows should encourage "learner judges" by allowing them to work with experienced officials. Here Mrs. Annabelle Francia-Kiss and young Robin Bergman compare their judges' cards.

good mover over a superior jumper, do so in every class. Then the rider knows what to emphasize in his preparation for showing before you.

One of the newer developments in judging is the numerical system. This would seem to be a practical way to assign a score to a horse or rider in a class over fences. With eight fences, generally, to be jumped one could give up to ten points per fence (total eighty) ten points for movement, and ten for general appearance and manners.

Judges differ in their reaction to the numerical system, which has been tried at some of the largest shows. Each judge assigns a numerical rating for the horse or rider, then results are tabulated, and an overall score is announced at the end of the performance. At a large show this enables exhibitors to know if they are high enough in scoring to remain near the ring for jogging their mounts preparatory to receiving ribbons, or whether they can put their horses away for the next class.

Others favor the system—and I am one of them—because it encourages audience participation. The spectator can mentally (or vocally) compare his own score with the judge's. He knows which horses are likely to be in the ribbons. He knows who has the highest score and what it will take to beat him for first place. At least one prominent judge feels, however, that the system turns up the six or eight best trips over fences, but not necessarily in the proper order. "A good judge selects and separates. If I give a number, then I'm letting the numbers sort themselves out," he contends. "Discussing it out between judges is a better method, I feel, although I've judged both by using numbers and using my regular system."

Hawkins feels the system is good if the "senior" judge breaks the ties in one class, the second-most "senior" judge does it in the next class, and so on. He feels it is especially good in equitation classes because riders can judge their own improvement and know how many points they are from placing in a class or how far behind the top rider they are. He believes it will be used in the AHSA Medal and ASPCA Maclay finals eventually.

But he also uses a system of columns, placing the best riders or horses in one column, the next best in another, and then putting pluses or minuses after riders in the same column. When it comes time to pin the class he quickly glances to the first column and—should he have less riders than ribbons to be awarded—then goes to the next column. This method would appear to have an advantage in a class where there are more entries than can be scored on one sheet of a judge's card.

Another young horsewoman who has exhibited in major shows for several years, and is just starting her judging career, asserts, "Everyone who shows should judge at least once. It's a great challenge and is a completely different view than you get from the saddle. You learn to keep your mouth shut when you are showing, you learn the importance of good riding manners.

"You see when a horse hangs a leg on a fence, you learn to make decisions. It's a lot different from watching from outside the ring. The hardest thing is to judge a small show. At the big shows there generally are five or so really good trips and no one seems to care as long as they all are in the ribbons. But at the little shows there are no really good trips. One horse has three bad fences out of eight, another horse also has three bad fences—but a different three.

"In a hack class, they sort themselves out. A green hunter class where horses aren't required to hand gallop is harder to judge. When they have to hand gallop, the horse that moves on has to win. That's why Striking won so many hunter under-saddle classes: he would move on and never blow up. Sometimes it's the overall impression and attitude that can win over a horse who is a better mover but tosses his head or commits another minor fault."

None of the many judges I've talked to over the years has ever mentioned having a system that assigns penalties to certain faults or weighs faults in ascending order of seriousness. Obviously, a knockdown is more serious than a rub, a hanging leg more serious than a "chippy" fence. All have their own types of "judge's shorthand" for marking the round over fences.

Brian Flynn believes the worst fault over fences is a dive, which is bad and dangerous, worse than stopping. He'd rather see a horse refuse than dive over a fence.

"You can't adopt hard and fast rules on something like a rub," he adds. "It can be a light rub that will knock off a rail that isn't too securely built into the fence, or it can be a hard knock—but the rail stays up. You have to use a little judgment in a case like that."

A "prop," when a horse gets in too close to the fence and has to arch himself almost straight up and down, usually will put a horse out of the ribbons—for inconsistency—in a good show. Jumping

199

"flat" across a fence usually will lead to another fault, such as a rub. Taking off over a fence off just one leg is dangerous and a major fault, Flynn adds.

"It's all in your mind's eye," he explains. "You don't want to see the horse's head up in the air, his mouth open. You want to see him under control, going smoothly—not leaving twenty feet away from one fence and two feet away from the next."

Mrs. Zander (Chris) Duffield admits, "There are some horses you don't like in the first class you see them. Then the next time they put in a good trip and you ask yourself, 'Why didn't I like him before?' But you can't let yourself have too much 'carryover' from one class to the next, you can't mark a horse on the basis of what he did before. However, you're bound to look twice at a horse you pinned first in a previous class. You expect him to do good. The horse that refused twice in the class before—you might not expect too much of him next time."

Mrs. Duffield finds it easier to judge a class over fences, when you are concerned only with one horse at a time, than an under-saddle class, when there are many horses passing the judge. "You have to glance down to write the number of the horse you like under saddle," she explains. "And, usually, as soon as you do, some horse—sometimes even the one you like—makes a mistake that you can't see." For that very reason, some judges like to judge such a class from outside the ring, where every horse is in front of them and none are behind them.

Flynn feels he has an advantage in not being involved in the horse business as a professional who buys and sells. "It's great not to owe anyone favors and just be objective," he says. "In some ways I'd like to see horse show judges have microphones around their necks, as the dairy cattle judges do, to explain what they like or dislike about a certain animal. I think it would help the young riders a lot, since you don't have time to talk to them all individually. Many times you can see their mistakes before they happen, just from their approach to a fence or the way they make their warm-up circle before starting their round. But maybe I just like to talk more than other judges."

Wayne Carroll, a noted Eastern horseman, uses the same symbols for an equitation over-fences class as he does for a hunter class. "A straight up and down fence can be caused by the rider getting ahead of the motion, leaning too far forward too soon," he explains, adding, "but on the flat, you just look at the overall

200

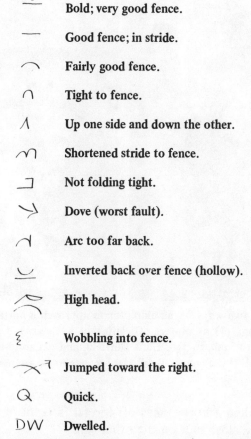

—	Bold; very good fence.
—	Good fence; in stride.
⌒	Fairly good fence.
∩	Tight to fence.
∧	Up one side and down the other.
⋂	Shortened stride to fence.
⌐	Not folding tight.
↘	Dove (worst fault).
⌐	Arc too far back.
∪	Inverted back over fence (hollow).
⌒	High head.
ξ	Wobbling into fence.
⤬	Jumped toward the right.
Q	Quick.
DW	Dwelled.

Symbols used by Mrs. Chris Duffield to mark her judge's card while scoring a class over fences.

picture and the rider's ability, weighing each situation as it comes about.

"If there are two possible approaches in an equitation over-fences class and one rider makes a great big circle and one a smaller circle, the latter should be counted as more of a plus for that rider because he is showing more skill."

Says Mervyn Alexander, a second-generation horseman who manages the Saddle and Bridle Club in Buffalo, New York: "What you're looking for all the time is consistency. Consistency in way of moving and consistency in the way of jumping.

"What you don't want to see is a dangerous fence, or a 'dive.'

201

There are two ways for an exhibitor to approach a horse show judge for an explanation: (1) at center, officiating as a steward, I give John Shaffner permission to talk to Mrs. Chris Duffield, and (2) an ill-mannered exhibitor, "portrayed" by Francis "Bob" Manley, has to be restrained from assualting the judge.

That's when a horse takes off too far in front of a fence and lands much too close to it on the other side.

"Then, too, a horse should get his thrust from his hind legs. Some of them jump off the forehand, which means they're throwing their front ends over and dragging the rest behind. Sometimes it takes you a while to figure out just what you don't like about a horse, and then it hits you—he's jumping off his front end.

"There's so much to judging, especially here in the East where we see—usually—so many good, consistent rounds that we often have to look for the 'little things' to make our decisions. They say you shouldn't consider a horse's conformation in a working hunter class, but you've got to be aware of it. If a horse has good conformation, you're going to enjoy looking at him more than a horse with poor conformation.

"There there's his attitude. If his ears are up and alert, it's a plus. If they're back, it's a minus. There was a horse named Daily

202

Nip that had won all over the country, but if it was really close, you'd probably have had to fault him because his tongue always hung out. He was a good jumper and it was only a bad habit, but it was unsightly. It'd probably be more of a fault in a hack class.

"Over a fence, you like to see a horse fold up his legs nicely. If he can get his toe about eight or ten inches from his elbow, that's just about perfect. The closer the toe comes to the elbow, the better it is. If they don't fold up well, then they're hanging their legs, which can be dangerous.

"A horse that folds up well isn't required to jump as high as a leg-hanger. The good-folding horse is jumping perhaps three-feet-seven or three-feet-eight inches to clear a three and one-half-foot fence. But the horse that doesn't fold up is jumping four feet to clear three and one-half feet, and that's got to take more out of him than the horse that 'uses himself' better.

"A bad corner on the hunter course can be forgiven if the horse jumps well, but if he moves smoothly on the corners and then props at his fences, it's a bad round. A lot of white in the eye is a

Judges Wayne Carroll (left) and Michael Page mark their cards before a class is pinned at the Washington, D.C., International Horse Show. *Photo by Sue Maynard.*

thing you don't like to see, but it's one of those 'tiny' faults, when you're forced to look for minor things because of the closeness of the more important abilities.

"What a hunter judge has to remember is that he supposedly is looking for a horse that would be the most agreeable mount to ride to hounds, on a fox hunt. Now it certainly isn't agreeable to ride a horse that lugs on the reins, or shortens stride before a fence or makes a big jump over a small fence.

"You have to take enough time to go to a hunter show and sit and watch and ask questions. In the old days, a clean round—getting around the course without any fences knocked down or refused—would pretty much get you into the ribbons. But that doesn't hold true in any good hunter show today. The competition has improved by leaps and bounds.

"And, of course, even though you are judging a hunter—in the big English shows—as a potential mount to hounds, you know he won't ever be in the hunt field until his show days are over. The difference between a 'hunting hunter' and a 'show hunter' is the same as the difference between a bench dog and a field trial dog. The commoner, less highly bred, less handsome field hunter has no real place in a show ring now, unless it's a little one-day show somewhere."

The new show judge, whether judging recognized or unrecognized shows, has a problem initially. He is best known in his home area. But if he has to begin judging there he has to judge his friends, enemies, former rivals, people who have helped him, horses he may have owned or shown or trained, and so on. If one can do a good job under such circumstances he is well on the way to a successful judging career. Still, it would be best to begin judging in a distant area, where one would be under much less pressure.

Even before accepting an invitation to judge, most experienced judges believe you should start out as a "guest" inside the ring while an experienced professional is doing the judging. Jack Frohm, a Rochester, New York, professional, advocates this approach. "You have to get inside the ring, not judge from the rail," he stresses. "And you can't do it for just one or two classes. You have to work the whole day, mark a card in every class, then have the judge and show manager and other officials go over it with you."

Steve Hawkins believes in starting at the smaller shows and

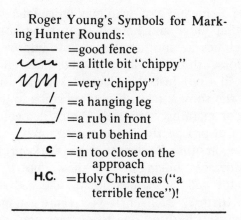

Roger Young's Symbols for Marking Hunter Rounds:

——— =good fence

〰 =a little bit "chippy"

〰〰 =very "chippy"

___/ =a hanging leg

___/ =a rub in front

∠___ =a rub behind

___c =in too close on the approach

H.C. =Holy Christmas ("a terrible fence")!

asking questions of top horsemen as a way of starting up the judging ladder. His first year he did three "C"-rated shows. The next year he did ten and in five years he was doing forty shows per year. But he didn't do an "A" show until he had been judging for three years.

"All things are relative," he said. "You may prefer a medium-strong pace, but sometimes a faster-moving horse has a much better round in all respects, and you have to pin him. If you have been around the circuit, the exhibitors have confidence in you. They know what you like and can almost pin the round with you.

"In conformation classes, by the way, you tend to go with a mature horse, and a horse reaches full maturity at six or seven years. The green conformation hunter class is one thing, but when the green hunter moves up into open competition the older horse, even with a few bumps, may have the better overall conformation than the younger horse because he has reached his maturity.

"You have to be as diplomatic as possible, yet remember that the exhibitors have paid their money to show under you and they have a right to deserve an explanation, if they ask it politely. You are helping in the sport of showing horses by educating them, by telling them how you think they can improve their horse's performance. A half-show, half-clinic is a fine way to do this. Often there simply isn't enough time at a large one-day show to explain your judging methods, much as you would like to.

"Some people have advocated judges, especially in conformation classes, using a microphone to explain their choices. This is done in a 4H livestock competition, for cattle, sheep, hogs, and other animals. I wouldn't like it in a horse show—a larger show, at any rate. Why? Someone else, who may judge later, could pick up a fault from that judge and hold it against the horse at another time. Judges' clinics are another good way to improve judging, and the various horse show divisions should have more of them.

"Then, too, it's not just the pleasant summer outdoor shows that comprise the show circuit. If you are going to judge you have to do the indoor marathons of twelve hours in a cold, drafty ring. That sours a lot of prospective judges very quickly."

Roger Young, another Rochester, New York, professional who has done considerable judging at "A" shows, notes, "You have to start off with the bad shows, bad horses, and bad rounds and let them separate themselves. Even if you can't get inside a ring at first, sit by yourself with no one to distract you, preferably at a big show, use a card, pick the horses one through eight, and then read your card back to a friend or a judge. Have good symbols so you can say 'He didn't change leads,' 'That one flicked his head over a fence,' 'That one dove.' If it's possible, compare your card to the judge's card. Be clear in your own mind how you separated the horses, but be open-minded when you discuss it with someone who knows more about it than you do. It might be good to pay your own transportation and lodgings to work with an experienced, cooperative judge at a good show.

"If you can read your card back to an exhibitor who questions you, you'll have no problems. The best way is to start small, learn how to do all the 'book work.' If you do a big show too soon, you'll get lost. And if you do get invited to an "A" show early in your judging career, be sure to work with an experienced judge. Two inexperienced judges sure can make a mess of things.

"On the other hand, many times the shows themselves are at fault and contribute to judging that is inferior to what the judges could do under proper circumstances. Too many shows run too long. The judges feel rushed, are out in the ring for too long at a stretch, they don't get a proper 'break' in the action, they aren't even offered a sandwich or coffee."

Young, too, would like to see more "semiprofessional" judges drawn from the ranks of former show riders who have professions or jobs unrelated to horses. "If you are operating a stable you can't take too many weekends off to judge because you have to take your horses and riders to compete at shows. Another problem is with judges who have been away from the show ring for a spell, perhaps training race horses. You have to keep 'your hand in' the game constantly. Most good judges want to do a small one-day show before a big 'A'-rated Spring show, just to get their 'eye' in shape. It's just like riding after being away from it for a while."

When interviewed, Roger Young was at an indoor, one-day winter show as a horseman, not a judge, but he pointed out: "I'm judging today, too, but I'm doing it mentally. You can't get out of practice if you're going to stay in the business.

"The thing to remember is to use your best judgment, and to be consistent. Judging horses is like anything else, it's one person's opinion. No one likes the exact same thing as someone else in clothing styles, hair styles, or automobiles. You can ask ten professional horsemen who they'd like to have judge them, and you'll get ten different answers.

"I don't think it's hard to keep friendship and judging separated. I have no hesitation in going out for dinner with other professional trainers and then judging their horses the next day. You don't even think of who is riding or showing the horse if you concentrate. When I come home and my wife asks me 'Who did well?' I usually answer 'A grey horse' or 'Number 77'—and not 'Rodney Jenkins's horse' or 'Joe Darby's horse.' You really can't remember if you're concentrating."

Jack Frohm agrees on professionals not being unanimous in their opinion of judges. He manages an "A" show, and when he asked them, most of his fellow professionals could not name three judges they would agree to show under.

As you gain experience, Frohm contends, you will learn to separate people who "buddy-buddy" you before a show and drop little hints about which horses they own that you will be judging. You will learn to overlook the obvious ways some professionals try to influence you from ringside.

"No judge wants to drop a horse down," he emphasizes. "You want them all to do well. You don't want to pin a bad horse or a bad round, but usually there aren't that many good performances. And you should be ready to pin immediately after the rounds over fences. You should have them right on your card. You shouldn't have to walk behind the horses and try to remember what number did something right or wrong during the class.

"And if you approach me after the class, I should be able to look at my card, show it to you, and explain just what your horse did. Fake excuses don't fool the public for long."

15 Judging Complaints: Western Style

That rumble you hear in the background at Western horse shows all over North America isn't just the sound of riders working their mounts. It's the rumble of discontent from exhibitors who are unhappy with the judging going on inside the show ring.

In some cases, the muttering and complaining is simply the "sour grapes" or "sour gripes" of riders whose horses were left out of the ribbons. This is human nature, although experienced show riders should be immune to that feeling after a season or two. In other cases it is the comments of new, "green" exhibitors who don't really know what the judge is looking for and think, after moving from backyard horse owner to show horse owner, that they are show-ring experts.

But in more and more cases the complaints are coming from veteran exhibitors who have been showing for many years, even decades. Many of them know enough to hold judge's cards themselves, and many of them do judge shows on occasion.

Anyone who has shown with any regularity, or who attends horse shows frequently, has seen or heard of incidents like the following:

"One stallion beat another seven straight times. The owner of the 'also-ran' gave him to a professional to show and now he's winning every time."

"I'm a breeder and I sold a good filly to an unknown amateur. I have another filly and show against him. I'm winning, he's not even in the ribbons, and he's getting disgusted with the whole thing. I know if I let my son show my filly and I showed his, she'd be placed no worse than third."

"We wanted to get a good judge from far away for our show. We got one from Texas. Our show's in New York—and here comes an exhibitor all the way from Texas just to show before his 'buddy' and pick up the points he needs."

"I've seen a show chairman stand up outside the ring to point out his two daughters to the judge in the ring."

"I've heard judges offered $500 to make a horse a grand champion at halter. It's worth it. The breeder makes it up in one stud fee."

"One judge told the kids in a halter class, 'Don't bother jogging.' He had the class pinned before they even came into the ring."

"I know of judges who have received commissions from professionals after the pros sold for big prices horses that these judges had consistently pinned first at shows."

Some of the problems have arisen strictly because of the growth of the number of Western horse shows, which have increased because more people own horses and want to try for ribbons with them. Because of restrictions on judges judging in the same states or geographical areas too often, shows are forced to go farther afield to find a judge. Often they hire a man simply because he is from far away, and don't bother checking with officials of shows where he has worked previously.

There also is a problem of more people coming into judging because there is a demand for judges and the pay is good. They are not really qualified but get the necessary recommendations from their friends, and proceed to make countless mistakes inside the ring.

The complaints against some judges center around their lack of knowledge in general and their failure to keep up to date on trends among the various breeds. These complaints are mostly about "halter" or "conformation" judging, and are prevalent at Western or breed shows for Quarter Horses, Appaloosas, Paints, Pintos, Palominos, Arabs, Morgans, and Saddlebreds.

There does seem to be general agreement, among those who disagree with judges, that judging of performance classes seems less subject to accidental or intentional error than conformation judging.

The other main complaint about judges falls under many headings, running from "political" to "payola," and concerns the "double standard," real or imagined, between amateur showmen and the professionals. According to this argument, the pros judge

209

A large halter class of top-quality Appaloosas poses a tremendous problem for a judge.

one week and show the next, so the one who is judging one weekend gives the edge to the pro who is judging him the next weekend. Others, who don't like the idea, are less vocal but still have the feeling that the professional horsemen are one big, cooperative "family" who virtually control the show ring's major winnings and leave scant pickings for amateurs.

Many of these exhibitors argue that the show associations have to be more stringent in judging judges. It should be harder for someone to become a judge. Once he is judging, the breed or show associations should regulate his actions more carefully, praising him when praise is due and criticizing or suspending him when his work is suspect. Also, the acknowledged top judges should not be seen again and again in the rings of the largest, highest-paying shows; good new judges should be able to rise to the top once they prove their capability.

Considering the variety of complaints, it is obvious there are no easy corrective measures to take. Yet the controversy continues, and some judges have been heard to state emphatically: "I'm pinning the professionals. I'm not going to cause any man to lose his job. If the pro doesn't win he's out of business; it's as simple as that." Other judges, "about two in one hundred," according to one veteran trainer, have turned the other way and are deliberately dropping pros out of the ribbons to encourage the amateurs with one or two "backyard" horses to stay in the showing game.

On the other hand, one top professional trainer who also judges contends, "A professional can get killed at the end of the day because the judge has used him too much previously. If I do well in showing a halter mare or stallion and I have a really good halter gelding, the judge will 'ding' him if he can."

Part of the problem concerns the relative "youth" of the Western breeds in the show ring. The American Quarter Horse Association was founded in the 1940s, other Western breed associations around the same time or later, and they are still in a process of growth and change. Unlike the short, heavily muscled "bulldog type" of Quarter Horse especially adept at quick starts and stops and having the "cow sense" needed for ranch work, today's Western breeds—and English, to a lesser extent—have become taller and more refined due to the introduction of Thoroughbred blood.

Timed classes in Western shows are a bit easier on the judge. Knocking down a barrel, for instance, is easy to observe and disqualifies horse and rider.

211

The Thoroughbred may have been crossed with the Quarter Horse solely to produce a better short-distance race horse originally, but the Quarter Horse has benefitted in other ways as a result—quicker responses to the rider's signals and a longer, more comfortable stride, in addition to size and refinement.

However, many Western judges have not kept abreast of the "modern Quarter Horse," or Paint, or Appaloosa, and still are pinning the "bulldog type" in halter classes. And according to Lou Pasquarella, a New York American Horse Shows Association judge for Western breeds: "Many 4-H riding clubs still are teaching that the 'bulldog type' is the ideal Quarter Horse. So when the kids and their parents graduate from 4-H shows to open shows, they think the judge is pinning the halter classes all wrong. They don't realize they are going from 'grammar school' to 'college' in quality of horses and degree of competition.

"But in some cases complaints are justified. I often see judges pin yearlings whose backs are higher than their withers. The judges say 'He'll grow out of it.' But all the rule books and veterinary conformation guides tell you that a horse must grow evenly; otherwise it's a structural weakness."

Many exhibitors are convinced that the best horses will not win ribbons until judges are prohibited from showing. One of them is an Eastern professional who, for obvious reasons, will remain anonymous. He explains:

"As big as showing has become, if a man wants to judge it should become a profession and he must do it full time. There is simply too much friction if he both judges and shows. If he's judging this week, then he's looking for a favor from the professional trainer who will be judging him the next weekend. Instead, he should be looking to do the very best job of judging he can, so that he will be asked to judge another show the following weekend.

"Trainers follow the judges they know to get points, and often you don't know if the horse earned the points on his conformation or performance or got them because his trainer was owed favors.

"The professionals usually do have the best horses. There are tremendous amounts of money behind some of them. How can you hope to beat a $35,000 horse with one you bought for $1,000? But there are occasions when the pro deserves to get 'knocked down' in the placings. They usually aren't.

"Let's face it—how big would shows be if there were only professionals in the ring? Not enough for 'A' ratings, that's for sure. We professionals need the 'little guy.' We should try to encourage them, not eliminate them. The amateur-owner or owner-rider class is one way.

"Too many judges somehow 'sneak in,' and they aren't active enough to really know what they are doing. There is no way to check on them, to know how good they are. They should be former showmen, so they are alert to the little tricks, like cutting off another horse in a pleasure class.

"At a show recently another pro asked me to lead in one of his halter mares for the judging of the grand champion. He took the shank of the younger mare, and I led in the older mare. Why? He knew which one was going to be named grand champion before we went in there. There wasn't that much difference between the two mares.

"In performance judging there's not as much room for individual preference or favors. It's too obvious, to the judge and to the people outside the ring, when the rider gets in trouble. The

A well-groomed horse and rider working smoothly through an imitation bridge obstacle in a trail horse class in an American Quarter Horse Association show. *Courtesy AQHA.*

good judge will afterwards tell you why you were second instead of first, while the poor judge will just give you a snippy answer or say, 'He had the better horse,' which is no answer at all.

"You learn to compete by experience, through the payment of entry fees as you go along. There is no way you can regulate how people spend their money. Youth Activity or Junior competition has gone beyond anyone's dreams. Who would ever think parents would spend so much for good horses, for trainers to take their children all over the country, to advertise the horse and rider's winnings in breed magazines?

"You can't blame the professional for taking the money and searching for points, for using any method he can to produce results. The average family can't compete with that; showing wasn't meant to be that way. Some people go along and get a better horse when they can afford it. But others drop out entirely."

"It should be much harder to become a judge," declared a long-time Morgan breeder. "I myself think it'd take another ten or twenty years of breeding Morgans before I'd consider myself qualified. But a man capable enough to make his living as a trainer, exhibitor, or breeder should make a good judge. And a true horseman who knows quality in one breed should be able to determine it in another, similar breed.

"I think there is quite a bit of conformation 'carryover' among Morgans, Arabs, and Saddlebreds—for example in head carriage and in the type of 'look' the breeders are aiming for. This is where I fault many of the judges. The class standards for a Park horse say the animal should be showy and animated and even have a 'show horse expression,' but the judges don't recognize it. They also fail to look at both ends of the horse to see the flexion in the hind legs.

"Morgan breeders, like most others, are now breeding for a taller horse. The old ideal was 14.1 to 15.1 hands but now it is closer to 15.1 or 15.2. We want to see the taller horses win, but we don't want size to be emphasized over quality, over a beautiful head and the head carriage that is a breed characteristic.

"As far as the 'professional courtesy' between pros goes, you either get truthful with yourself and admit you need a better horse and more riding or training ability yourself, or a professional to help you or show for you, or you get mellower and become more selective about where and before whom you show."

Miss Joan Tolhurst of Rochester, New York, who holds an AQHA judge's card, believes the main problem is the increasing number of exhibitors. "When you have forty horses in the ring and only six ribbons," she said, "how can everyone be happy with the outcome?

"Yes, the big trainers usually win. But if people would honestly analyze it, they would have to agree that they usually have the best horses. If the best horse isn't pinned, it hurts the show. Youth classes are harder to win than open classes. How can a person with one or two horses in the backyard beat the child whose parents pay top dollar for a horse, equipment, and training? You can see the difference when they come into the ring; the youngster with the best equipment and smartest, best-fitting clothes simply stands out. A good amateur with lots of ring mileage can compete with the professionally trained rider, but the average rider cannot."

One of the problems in Western breed shows is the wide variety of classes, Western and English, that are held. Many Western judges simply don't know what an "English pleasure horse" is and how he should perform. It is almost as preposterous when these men try to judge Quarter Horse "working hunters."

An English pleasure horse is generally a taller, more refined example of the breed, whether it be Quarter Horse, Appaloosa, Paint, or Palomino. He should move with a longer stride, and cover ground at the trot, not simply jog along like the Western pleasure horse. But many judges pin the "sleepy moving" horse in both English and Western pleasure classes.

Hunter-jumper trainers who have occasion to see Quarter Horse judges pinning hunter classes have a sure cure: "Ship all Quarter Horse judges east for a month or two and have them sit at ringside and learn what a good hunter looks like."

One local judge who works as a ring steward at many big Quarter Horse shows in New York state comments: "Most of the judges mean well, but they really don't know what they are doing. They usually look very relieved when I tell them I'm a hunter-jumper judge and simply tell me, 'Go ahead, you pin the class.' Many of them try to learn what hunter judging is all about. They will stay right in the ring with me, watch how I score the class, and ask questions.

"One fellow thought, after watching me score a few horses going around, that he was ready to do it himself. So I let him. After all, he was the one who was getting the judge's paycheck.

Judges who pin Appaloosa men's costume class have to be history experts as well as top horsemen. The authenticity of the costume is as important as its effect.

But what happened? He pinned a horse first that broke from a canter to a trot to change leads between fences."

Dr. Robert Rost, a top Eastern show judge and designer of hunter and jumper courses, manages several large shows that include divisions for hunters and Quarter Horses. "I try to get a hunter judge and Quarter Horse judge together in the ring," he said, "and they should be able to learn from each other. But often, at other shows, Quarter Horse judges ask for help in judging hunter classes and there's no help around.

"The American Horse Show Association rule book spells it out—pace, manners, and jumping ability. This means going quietly, because you're looking for good manners, but the horse has to have some brilliance, too, not the 'dead quiet' lope you see in Western pleasure classes."

A hunting pace means a fluid, ground-covering gallop with as little wasted motion as possible. There should be no tossing of the head, fighting the bit, speeding up or slowing down, or breaking into a trot to change leads.

216

"A good movie would help the Quarter Horse judges," Dr. Rost believes. "The AHSA has a hunter movie that would help them quite a bit. So would good courses. AQHA rules require only four different fences jumped a total of eight times. Fences should be solid-looking to make the horse jump better. Flimsy poles are dangerous."

D. Jerry Baker, another hunter-jumper professional who has designed many international-type Grand Prix jumping courses, warns: "Jumping tends to make Quarter Horses, or Thoroughbreds, bullish and rank. You have to be careful and know what you are doing. You can't just put a rail up and force them over it. A horses's jumping muscles must be developed; he must be suppled.

"When it comes to building courses, you could have the best course designer in the world build your jumps and still have a terrible class, because the course designer may assume the horses have a certain level of training and ability and therefore build a course that is too difficult. It is better to have someone who knows the type of horses that will be competing and can build a course within their range of capability. Good courses are based on the average galloping stride of the horse, and obviously the Quarter Horse's stride is going to be shorter than that of the Thoroughbred."

Many hunter-jumper horsemen believe that if Quarter Horses and other Western breeds are shown under English tack and in English-type classes, there should be classes for English equitation, too. How can a rider perform well in English pleasure or over fences, let alone train his horse for such events, if he doesn't have the proper seat on the horse? they ask. And how can the rider develop that proper seat unless he is judged on his riding form and competes against others? Although the AQHA had approved classes or point championships in such "exotic" classes as cutter and chariot racing, pleasure driving and dally roping for several years, it did not add a youth class in English horsemanship until 1977.

Miss Tolhurst admits the Western judges' weaknesses in this area, but points out: "We're just beginners in the English area, most of us. Most judges, especially from the West, haven't been exposed to it before. But give us time. After all, what would a hunter-jumper judge do if all of a sudden they decided to have Thoroughbreds compete in reining or roping classes?"

Some exhibitors feel it might be best if judges were assigned to shows by breed headquarters and their names kept secret. Then there would be less phone-calling to judges during the days leading up to shows, and less following of judges to shows by their friends. If the organizations, through feed-back by state or district chapters and exhibitors, could develop a select group of top judges, it could keep them busy judging and end the judge-show-man conflict.

This is just one possibility. Another could be the rating of judges as "acceptable" or "unacceptable" by breed associations. State groups could demand that their national organization bar all judges who have not judged a required number of shows within a period of years. National organizations could be required to publish complaints against judges, or to suspend—if not bar—judges guilty of improper behavior or just poor work.

As Western and breed shows become larger, and as the quality of horses and riders improves, the quality of the judging must improve also. There simply is too much verbal "smoke" from exhibitors to ignore the possibility of "fire" in the middle of the ring.

16 Improving Your Horse Show

Horse shows are wonderful. They offer a visual treat to the eyes of spectators. They offer a close-up look at the objects of the affections of hundreds of horse-crazy youngsters. They are a weekly ritual for the competitors, a chance to renew friendships and competition. For the professional, they are the culmination of a week spent trying to improve his riders and their mounts, and discovering whether he has succeeded or not.

But no matter what the show, from the simplest "back yard" type to the huge Class "A" extravaganza, one can always be sure to hear the same comment: "This show is running too long." As more and more people compete in more and more shows, the novelty of spending ten to twelve hours per day at a show ground begins to wear thin. And one doesn't have to go to too many shows before he can recognize the "dead spots," when time drags and nothing seems to be moving, when competitors and spectators simply are sitting around with nothing to occupy themselves. How many cups of coffee and hot dogs can one digest?

As the sponsor/organizer of a horse show, you owe it to the participants to keep them as happy as you can. If you make no effort to improve your show you'll soon lose entries to other, better-run shows. Fewer entries mean less profit, or less money raised for charity—the two usual reasons for staging a horse show in the first place.

Do most shows make money? Of course. Figure it out. Twenty entries, at three dollars each, in an equitation class. Income, sixty dollars. Outgo, three to four dollars for ribbons and a portion of the costs for the judge and other paid officials. Incidentally, the most profitable type of show to run would be an all walk-trot-

The goal of every young hunter-jumper rider: the Olympic Games. This is the individual show jumping course for the 1976 games in Bromont, Quebec. *Photo by Sue Maynard.*

canter affair. Any horse can compete, any rider can manage the class routine of "green pleasure horse," "open pleasure horse," "novice road hack," "limit horsemanship," and so on. Everyone has a chance to win, and all the show committee can do is count the profits. But I digress.

You can't forget the "walk-trot-canter" group because they can put your show comfortably over the break-even point financially. What you want to do is arrange your show program so that class can follow class in rapid order, riders can be kept aware of what class is upcoming, and as little time as possible is spent with all competitors outside the ring waiting for fences to be altered or rearranged or barrels or trail class obstacles to be set up.

This is done in three ways, each separate but all three working together: a well-planned class schedule, hunter or jumper courses set up to be used for several classes in succession, and an experienced horse show announcer who knows how to help things move along. Since I've frequently found myself behind the microphone I may overestimate the importance of this job at times, but bear with me.

A good announcer puts in as long a day as any show official. He should be at the grounds at least a half-hour before the show

220

begins. He may even have time for two cups of coffee while he announces: that entries should be made as soon as possible; what classes will be first on the program; when the ring or hunt course will be closed for schooling; that the refreshment booth is open; where course diagrams are posted; the location of the entry booth; and the license numbers of improperly parked cars and vans. Then he can begin his countdown to the first class.

Somewhere early in the show there is bound to be a discrepancy noted in the printed program, and this must be corrected over the loudspeaker. By then the announcer is settled into a more comfortable rut: announce the class in the ring, remind competitors about the upcoming class; relay information about whether there is to be a lunch (or dinner) break (it should be up to the judge if the show is running long); and remind people where the entry booth, refreshment stand, and lavatories are located. (Sometimes he even has a moment to locate one of the latter himself, just as long as he isn't gone too long.)

Courses should be posted where riders will have an opportunity to study them well before the time the class is to begin. Mac Cone and Brendan Damon are doing just that at the Ox Ridge Horse Show. *Photo by Sue Maynard.*

221

Some of the biggest time-wasters at shows are riders who are afraid to enter the ring first, particularly in a class over fences. The rider isn't always sure of the course, he may not be completely ready. As a friend, I sympathize with him. But as an announcer I'm ready to crucify him! He's the one who adds minutes to the show that become an hour or more by the end of the day.

The announcer can't cure the laggard himself. He needs the approval of the judge and the show manager to: (1) call the first number on his list of the class's competitors and give him one minute to get into the ring or be disqualified, or (2) give a rider an extra point—assuming the judge is using the numerical system—or a "plus" for being the first one in the ring. This especially is useful in getting riders into the ring promptly for Medal and Maclay classes. It usually takes only one disqualification, in the first class, to get riders into the ring promptly. I also have found it advantageous to call out the first few numbers on the class list at the start of each class, to get them—or someone else entered by the same trainer—into the ring quickly.

Many trainers used golf carts to save walking, or running, between outside courses, rings, and schooling areas at major horse shows. John Shaffner and Beth Snyder watch a class at the Lake Placid Show. *Photo by Sue Maynard.*

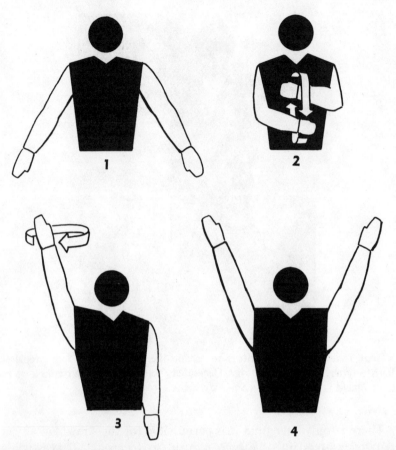

Good communications between ringmaster and announcer depend on signals that are easy to see and cannot be mistaken for each other. Some examples are: (1) walk; (2) trot or jog; (3) canter or lope; and (4) come in and line up, facing the ringmaster.

Good communication between the judge, or ringmaster, and the announcer also can save a few seconds per class that later add up to minutes. I do not feel the signals of one finger for "walk," two fingers for "trot;" et cetera, are good ones. A finger is too small an object to catch the eye of an announcer sitting one hundred feet away. I prefer bold, flamboyant gestures that one cannot miss or misinterpret.

It also helps if you ask the judge beforehand whether in a walk-trot-canter type class, for instance, he likes to try to "fool" the riders or just follows the "walk, trot, canter, reverse, walk, trot, canter" routine. This can save you another few seconds.

223

A tent that allows competitors to escape the summer heat is appreciated. Beth Snyder, mounted on Miss December, watches a rival on course at the Lake Placid Show. *Photo by Sue Maynard.*

There is only one time it is permissible for the show announcer to take matters into his own mouth, so to speak. That is when there is a class in the ring working together and one rider obviously is out of control, or about to fall off. "Stop and stand please" is the correct announcement. The horse may settle down if all movement ceases. Certainly he will be easier to catch if he throws his rider. Such incidents are few, especially at the larger shows, but an alert announcer often can prevent a serious injury.

Other time savers, that should be approved by the judge and show manager, are: elimination for major faults in some classes (usually open or junior hunters, not in green classes); having horses observed for soundness as they trot into and out of the ring, rather than having them jog separately before ribbons are awarded; and opening the ring gates to have the next class file into the ring while the previous class winners are receiving their ribbons. Using all of these practices should save several minutes in each class.

A good announcer can serve show management in another way,

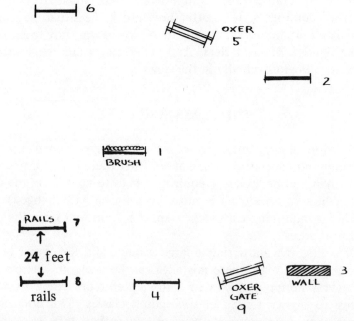

A hunter course that can be used for several classes without making changes (except for height), designed by Debbie Shaffner.

Course No. 1—Jump, in order, fences 1, 2, 3, 4, 5, 6, 7, 8, 9.

Course No. 2—Jump, in order, fences 1, 3, 2, 9, 8, 7, 6, 5.

Course No. 3—Jump, in order, fences 1, 3, 2, 6, 7, 8, 9, 5.

For a horsemanship class, requiring two changes of direction, such as an ASPCA Maclay Class, jump, in order, 1, 2, 3, 4, 5, 9, 8, 7, 6. For another such class, say an AHSA Medal class, jump, in order, 1, 9, 5, 4, 3, 2, 6, 7, 8.

also. He can check each horse performing in a class against the master class list. It is amazing how often, especially in a one-day show, riders compete in a class without being properly entered through the entry booth. A good follow-up can mean fifteen to fifty dollars per day in entry fees that otherwise might never be paid.

Near the show's end, of course, the announcer begins reminding competitors to settle their accounts at the entry booth. His final job is to thank everyone for coming to the show.

Announcers at horse shows are simply communicating informa-

225

tion to spectators and competitors. One must refrain from "clever" comments, no matter how much the situation seems to lend itself to humor. You are there to inform, not to entertain. Make it brief. Make it clear. And never, never talk while someone is performing individually in the ring.

THE CLASS SCHEDULE

Far too many horse show schedules are drawn up with seemingly no advance planning at all. First there is a pleasure horse class, then a jumper class, (requiring fences to be built in the ring), then a hunter class (fences must be lowered and changed), then another nonjumping class (fences must be removed from the ring). And so it goes.

Of course if a show ring is large enough, and the course builder experienced enough, these mistakes can be avoided. There should be several jumping classes in a row, preferably going from low fences to higher fences in succeeding classes. The nonjumping classes should be grouped together, since they take less time to judge and many horses will be going in more than one of them.

I do not think it is a good idea to start off a show with a hunter under-saddle, pleasure horse, or equitation on the flat class. Most horses coming off vans early in the morning are in a frisky mood. It would be much better if they worked that friskiness off in a class or two over fences before they are asked to exhibit perfect manners on the flat, and in company with other horses.

A similar situation exists for open jumpers. It might be better to offer a hunter class or two that jumper riders—in the smaller shows—would be able to use as a warm-up for their horses before facing them at the higher, wider jumps.

With shows growing larger and larger, there have been some efforts made to schedule classes for groups of riders one after the other, so the group can finish showing within a reasonable time and leave for other activities or home. One method is to hold—for example—all the junior hunter classes and then the more advanced equitation classes in the morning. Classes for children's hunters and the limit or beginner horsemanship classes would be held in the afternoon. This is probably more helpful during the fall and winter indoor shows, which get rather boring for one and all. In the summer, in the good weather, no one usually is in as much of a

JUMPER COURSE

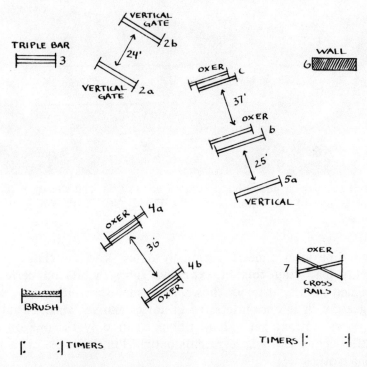

A jumper course that can be used for several classes, without fences being changed, designed by Debbie Shaffner.

Class 1—Fences, in order, 1, 2a, 2b, 3, 4a, 4b, 5a, 5b, 5c, 6, 7. Jump-off Order—1, 3, 2a, 2b, 6, 7.

Class 2—Fences 1, 5a, 5b, 5c, 6, 7, 2a, 2b, 3, 4a, 4b. Jump-off Order—1, 5a, 5b, 5c, 6, 2a, 2b, 4a, 4b.

Class 3—Fences 1, 4b, 4a, 3, 5c, 5b, 5a, 2a, 2b, 6, 7. Jump-off Order—1, 4b, 4a, 3, 6, 7.

hurry to leave. Similarly, in a Western show, all "working" classes could be held in the morning, all "games" classes in the afternoon. Or all the junior classes in the morning, all the "open" classes in the afternoon.

Although it makes sense to schedule the types of classes that have proved to be the most popular at other shows in the area, most riders and spectators get bored doing and seeing the same

One of the newest hunter-jumper shows in the East, and already acknowledged as one of the finest, is at Lake Placid, New York. *Photo by Sue Maynard.*

thing time after time. I personally detest lead-line class, where parents lead tiny tots in expensive riding habits on perfectly groomed ponies, at major shows. At a small show, it's a good way to get the little ones interested in horses and showing. I'd rather see every entrant get a blue ribbon than only the one on the prettiest pony and whose parents bought him the most attractive riding clothes.

Providing there's enough interest, or maybe as a means of sparking interest, I would like to see more family-type classes: parent-child, on the flat and over fences; a family class where as many family members as know how to ride scramble aboard horses with somewhat matching coat colors; and a class for family pairs: brother-brother, sister-sister, sister-brother, and parent-child.

Among other classes I've seen only on occasion, but felt were of more than passing interest, were: pairs of hunters, providing fences are wide enough; tandem hunters, one preceding the other until halfway around the course, when they switch positions; nonowner riders on borrowed or school horses; best-groomed horse; and jumper relay classes where one rider completes the course and passes his whip to his partner.

Classes for "teams" of jumpers representing one stable or a geographical region are becoming increasingly popular and also could be held on the local level. These mainly have been held as jumper classes, but a similar competition for hunters—judged on a numerical basis—would seem to be worthwhile. In this day of women's liberation, "boys" against "girls" teams seem overdue. And why not "youth" against those over thirty years of age? If you have a combination English-Western show, why not a "challenge" class, with the English riders competing over trail class obstacles, for example, and the Western riders competing over jumps? Try to show a little creativity, but don't go overboard.

A typical two-day indoor show schedule, with classes for the same group of riders following each other as closely as possible.

Saturday, 9 A.M.

1. Limit Equitation, over fences.
2. Children's Hunter, over fences.
3. Children's Hunter, over fences.
4. Children's Hunter, over fences.
5. Children's Hunter, under saddle.
6. Pleasure Horse.
7. Limit Equitation, flat.
8. Open Equitation, flat.
9. Junior Hunter, under saddle.
10. Junior Hunter, over fences.
11. Open Jumper, Table I.
12. ASPCA Horsemanship.
13. Junior Hunter, over fences.
14. AHSA Medal.
15. Open Jumper, Table II, Section 2.
16. Open Jumper, Table II, Section 2.

Sunday, 9 A.M.

17. Amateur-owner Hunter, over fences.
18. Amateur-owner Hunter, over fences.
19. Amateur-owner Hunter, under saddle.
20. Limit Hunter, over fences.
21. Limit Hunter, over fences.
22. Limit Hunter, over fences.
23. Junior Hunter, over fences.
24. Green Hunter, over fences.
25. Green Hunter, over fences.
26. Green Hunter, over fences.
27. Green Hunter, under saddle.

REMEMBERING THE PUBLIC

If you hope to attract the general public to your show, it is best to plan your schedule of classes to have your most interesting or exciting classes at the times you would expect to have the largest number of spectators. Under normal conditions this would be about 11 A.M. to around 1 P.M., from 3 to 6 P.M., and from 7 to 9 P.M.

For some reason there always has been a tendency to hold the open jumper classes, generally the most exciting to the spectator, as the last event on the program—morning, afternoon, or evening. Since the first wave of spectators will arrive around the lunch hour, a late-morning feature class is fine. But one late in the afternoon runs into the problems of young children becoming tired, parents becoming bored, the approaching dinner hour, and evening activities of another nature, such as Little League baseball.

An evening program of two or three hunter classes before a jumper class is likely to find a deserted grandstand by the time the jumper class begins, due to a combination of boredom and approaching bedtimes for young spectators. If your horse show is receiving any type of newspaper or television coverage, holding the jumper class in midafternoon guarantees adequate light for photographers. Few lighted horse show arenas, indoors or out-doors, are bright enough for television cameras, and many riders object to flashbulbs or other bright lights used by still photographers. In addition, a late-evening jumper class may be held too late for a newspaper's deadline, and its results will not be included in the next day's story about the show. Hopefully, a well-written story of Wednesday's exciting jumper class will attract more spectators to Thursday's program.

The public also must be considered when it comes to refreshments and toilet facilities. Hire an outside caterer who is knowledgeable about what food to offer and has his own cooking and refrigerating equipment if your show does not have proper equipment of its own. If you are running your own stand, be sure you have plenty of soft drinks and ice to keep them cold in both summer and winter, lots of hot coffee, and hot chocolate in the winter. Hot dogs are not an imaginative item, but are easy to prepare. Have plenty of straws, napkins, and coffee stirrers, and the largest trash barrels you can find at the refreshment stand, in the seating areas, and at ringside. Separate lavatories are a

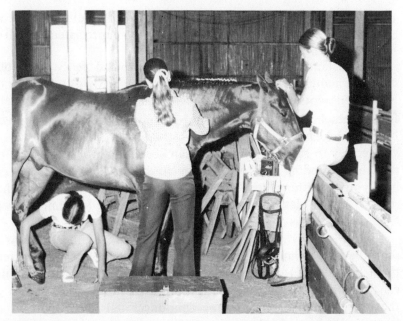

There's nothing like a couple of extra pairs of hands to help get a horse ready for a class. *Courtesy AQHA.*

necessity, and rented portable units might be preferable to having the general public trooping through your lounge and/or stables to use permanent facilities.

If your riding establishment offers lessons or trail riding to the general public it is only common sense to have printed material available near the refreshment stand, or perhaps passed out by your younger riders. I've never seen it done, but a steady old school horse under the supervision of an older teenager for free or moderate priced "rides" for tiny or older children would seem to be a good method of attracting new riding students. An enterprising youngster with an instamatic camera and another holding the steady school horse ought to make a profit for himself and many friends for your stable—but check with your insurance agent first.

A little effort by show management can make jumper classes even more interesting than they already are by giving spectators some indication of just how high the fences are. This would appear to be quite simple and involve little effort—just make some type of mark on the white-painted jump standard to indicate height. There could be a solid black line with a "5" below it to indicate five feet, and so on. This information also would be appreciated by horse show reporters.

The distance between elements of a spread fence probably could be indicated by a cardboard sign with arrows at either end. Such signs could resemble the ones used at track meets, where figures can be substituted simply by flipping the face of the sign over to a new number.

Needless to say, the announcer can keep spectator interest at its peak by reminding everyone how many horses have gone clean or by saying something like "five faults or less are needed to be in the ribbons in this class." An automatic timing device for jump-offs or time classes also is an asset.

Hunter classes usually comprise most of the horse show's schedule and, in my opinion, offer a real challenge as far as making them interesting for new—and old—spectators. The only way this can be done is to do away with the practice of announcing only the horse's number and let the announcer tell the name of the horse and rider and a little about their past achievements, if any, as they gallop around the course.

At present only the number is given on the somewhat nonsensical notion that if the rider's or horse's name is announced it could unduly influence the judge. How silly! If the judge didn't know the riders or horses his ignorance would last just one class. Then, when the first class winners are announced, he would know who the best local riders are and—supposedly—keep them in the ribbons the rest of the show. I just don't believe that with air travel and the busy schedule of the best horse show judges it is possible to bring a judge into an area "cold" and expect him not to know any of the horses or riders.

On the other hand, many spectating families or groups buy only one program at a show. Junior may have the program when a horse starts a round that Mama may want to watch. If the announcer tells her the horse is "Madison Square Garden champion," ridden by Mr. Gold Medal winner, then certainly that round is going to be of more than casual interest to her. But if it's just "Number 405 now on course," can you blame anyone for being bored?

My last suggestion for improving spectator appeal has to do with the "scoreboard." In most athletic events, the score is the most important factor and always in a place of prominence. At horse shows the standings for championships in the various divisions are usually kept in the secretary's booth or some other equally inaccessible location.

Why can't this information be displayed prominently? When the show's leading hunter comes into the ring, why can't the announcer tell the spectators, "This horse can clinch the show championship with a first or a second in this class?" Would this tend to influence the judge? I doubt that it would since the horse's rider, owner, and riders and owners of the other contending horses all know the point situation. Why keep the other spectators in the dark? I believe the same situation should be emphasized in jumper classes, too, and can be done without worrying about possibly influencing the judge.

The first horse show to follow some of these suggestions will earn spectators' undying gratitude.

17 Publicizing Your Horse Show

How do you attract spectators to a horse show? Thousands of dollars in prize money, a well-arranged schedule of classes, and the presence of Rodney Jenkins, Kathy Kusner, Frank Chapot, and David Broome won't draw a crowd if the general public doesn't know about it. This means your show committee must learn how to deal with the media: newspaper sports editors and television news and sports directors.

Notice I mentioned newspaper "sports editors," not "society editors." The biggest mistake most horse show publicity chairmen make is arranging to have a group of smiling committee ladies and their sweet daughters and their horses staring vacantly into the camera on the society or women's pages. I feel the sports pages have much higher readership among the general public, and a horse show really is athletic competition—and belongs on the sports pages.

Most sports reporters and newspaper readers are "team sport" oriented, and few understand what horse shows are all about. And if the reporter doesn't really understand his subject then it's going to be hard for him to write an interesting story that—hopefully—will attract Mr. and Mrs. General Public, and their children, away from their television set and out to your show grounds. The simple solution is to hire a working newsman to spend his off-duty time writing stories about your show prior to its opening class.

Most reporters are happy to pick up some extra money and—let's face it—editors would rather have an interestingly written story that meets their standards than a story written free by a superb rider who doesn't know the first requirement of a news story. The working reporter has friends in the media too.

They may stretch a point and use his story as a favor to him. They rarely owe any favors to, or are personally acquainted with, the members of the show committee.

A good reporter will ask enough questions of you, the show chairman, or the show manager so that he will find out something that he thinks will interest his readers. He's a professional at writing interesting stories, so just let him work—although you can offer suggestions when appropriate.

What is interesting to newspaper readers? Money, for one thing. A $10,000 Grand Prix or stakes class automatically captures the eye (or ear, in case of television news). A total of $20,000 in prize money for the complete show isn't a bad figure to toss around. If you have three hundred horses entered figuring each one is worth around $2,000, you have a phrase like "Show horses with a combined value of $500,000." Now that's an attention-grabber!

Names make news, too, and if your show expects any of the leading professionals or U.S. Equestrian Team riders—past or present—to appear, you have another important ingredient for getting the public's attention.

A properly worded publicity release might read as follows:

Contact: Charles Harland
Office 727-9100
Home 442-4356

Michael Page, winner of nine Olympic and Pan American Games medals, will judge the Foxcatcher Farm Horse Show, which will begin at 9 A.M. Sunday, May 5, at the showgrounds, 9700 Center Rd., Rochester, Minn.

Mr. Page, of New York City, competed in the three-day event, considered the most demanding equestrian sport, on an international level from 1959 to 1968. He was individual Gold Medal winner in the 1959 and 1963 Pan American Games and won a team Gold Medal and a Bronze Medal for finishing third as an individual in the 1967 games.

In Olympic competition, Page won team Silver Medals at Tokyo in 1964 and in Mexico in 1968 and an individual Bronze in Mexico. At Tokyo he was fourth as an individual, missing a Bronze Medal by one-fifth of a point.

Now working full-time in advertising, Page is much in demand as a horse show judge all over the nation. He also found time to coach Canada's Three-Day Event team on a part-time basis for the Montreal Olympic Games.

The show will offer championships in four hunter divisions—junior, limit, children's, and amateur-owner—and in open and amateur-owner jumpers. Classes also are scheduled in horsemanship and for pleasure horses.

The featured $500 Open Jumper Stake is scheduled for 3 P.M.

All of the above is news.

The Sunday show is the first of the season at Foxcatcher Farm's new outdoor show ring, considered one of the most complete facilities in the Midwest. Show manager is John P. Doolin, owner of Foxcatcher. Admission will be $2 for adults and $1 for children. Reserved parking spaces are $5 and can be reserved by calling 838-1490.

All of the last paragraph is publicity; the ticket information more properly should be contained in a paid advertisement.

The newspaper definition of an expert, by the way, is "anyone from out of town." Which means you ought to forget about publicizing local riders if at all possible, unless one of them owns a horse that won the hunter championship at Madison Square Garden or the Washington International the previous season. The visiting stars usually have a bit more glamour than the local professionals that perform every month at the regular unrecognized shows.

If your show is in August, June wouldn't be too soon to visit your local newspaper. Some have color sections that are prepared five or six weeks in advance. Usually these sections have stories that utilize five or more pictures. But again, you have to have a good "story line" to tie it all together.

A picture is worth one thousand words, but not if the editor doesn't use it. Every horse owner has dozens of pictures of himself and his horse over the top of a fence, or executing a nice sliding stop. The only problem with such pictures is that they nearly always require three columns of newspaper space—and are so common that many sports editors are sick of seeing them. Another problem is that the pictures generally were taken last show season and the horse now is owned by someone else (or lame). There's nothing an editor likes better than to run a picture of a horse or rider who never do compete in the show.

So, let's look for a variety of photos. A "one-column" wide size means close-ups of a pretty girl or a properly attired male holding a braided, trimmed horse by the reins. A two-column wide picture might be a rider bandaging the legs of his top jumper, or simply sitting in the saddle (the photo taken from an angle in front), or a trainer (standing) talking to a mounted rider. We'll include a few horses jumping fences, too. And each will have the name of the horse and rider on the back and some other typewritten information, attached by a paper clip or tape, such as the rider's address and the dates and time and location of the show.

I think advance publicity should eliminate pictures and any mention of junior riders. If this is a sports event that requires skill and has an element of danger to it—which it does—then how can little children be a part of it? That's the thinking of the average sports fan. So let's not try to capture his attention with pretty hunter ponies jumping two foot fences. And by eliminating all the junior riders—except, of course, any who have won major championships at Devon or Madison Square Garden and the like—the show chairman is spared countless explanations to unhappy parents and is able to keep most instructors sullen but silent.

A pretty girl (Jayne Schutt) and a handsome horse (One For The Road). What sports editor could resist using this picture? *Courtesy t. h. e. Studio; photo by Ken Schmidt.*

237

Advertising is different from publicity. Advertising is something the show must pay for. It is obvious. It advertises the show's dates, times of performances, admission prices. A news story, or publicity, will mention time and place, but not much more.

Advertising for a horse show probably belongs in the movie/theater page of a newspaper. The ad should catch the reader's eye—a picture of a horse jumping a fence rather than just a horse's head, for instance. Names make news, and they also help ads. If you have Rodney Jenkins or Frank Chapot entered in your show, your ads should mention the fact. People will come to see names they have read in newspapers. The names of other riders, no matter how well known to regular show fans, mean nothing to the Average Sports Fan. And those are the folks your show is trying to attract. But if your show doesn't have the big names that everyone knows, then you have to make lesser names known to the Average Sports Fan through publicity, through frequent exposure in newspapers and on radio and television stations in the weeks leading up to the start of your show.

Another area of the newspaper that frequently can be utilized for show publicity purposes is that belonging to the various newspaper columnists. The history of your show's oldest trophy, a rider riding in his first show since a bad spill, a horse that's a half-brother to a famous racer—these are the type of "offbeat" features a columnist looks for. Mr. Local Pro declaring "TV cowboys can't ride" might even interest the entertainment editor.

As to the show itself, your first story might deal with the selection of judges. Any judge worthy of being hired ought to be able to furnish the show chairman with an up-to-date biography of his riding, training, and judging background, and furnish a decent picture also. (But few do!)

The next story might be about a new division in the show, a new trophy, or added money going to an all-time high. But let's not let our imaginations run away with us when predicting how many entries will be made!

Now might be the time to start dividing up your publicity, if you are hoping for space in more than one newspaper. Sending one editor a carbon copy of the story already printed in another paper won't win you many friends. If you have two competing papers, why not concentrate all your hunter publicity in one and your jumper stories in the other? If you're dealing with smaller papers, try to feature a rider in their circulation area who'll be tackling the "big names." Try to give each paper some exclusive information.

Television is a different matter entirely. Here everything must be geared to the eye. Luckily horses and riders are very photogenic and make good feature items for news broadcasts. A training session of riders working over jumps around the show ring at one of the area stables is a good idea. So is a group of committee members painting and cleaning the show grounds, as long as there are a few horses nearby. Sometimes the stables and show grounds are too far for the station's photographers, however, and you must be prepared to furnish your own film clips in order to get good "play" on television.

If it is possible to have a horseman interviewed on radio or television be sure to equip him, and the announcer, with a basic fact sheet listing the hours of each performance, the exact location of the show, and admission charges. You'd be surprised how even

The horse (Third Chance) is folding up nicely, the rider (Diane Murray) is in good position, but somehow there isn't too much thrilling about a picture of a hunter in action. *Courtesy t. h. e. Studio; photo by Ken Schmidt.*

But a jumper soaring high over an imposing fence, as Jason is doing here for Debbie Shaffner, is a picture with much more eye appeal for the average newspaper editor or sports-page reader. *Courtesy t. h. e. Studio; photo by Ken Schmidt.*

the most glib "Mr. Personality" can freeze up under pressure and get tongue-tied. Most women riders are better conversationalists than their male counterparts, I've found. Too many men are like Rodney Jenkins, masters of understatement who describe an Idle Dice simply as "a nice horse."

A week before the show, you should be able to find out if the local newspaper is going to assign a reporter to cover the show personally or is going to expect someone to phone in or drop off the results each night. You should also be able to get a firm commitment if a photographer is going to be assigned, and at what time he'll appear.

From both a publicity and a spectator's standpoint, the jumpers should be in a featured position in the program. If the morning newspaper is going to send a photographer, he'll probably be coming early in the evening. If you have a junior hunter class with forty entries scheduled then, Mr. Photographer isn't going to get a very thrilling picture.

A photo of a twelve-year-old rider taking a three-foot fence, perfect form or not, isn't going to attract the attention of Mr. Average Sports Fan and bring him, Mrs. ASF, and their children to the show the next day. A picture of Mr. Pro clearing five and a half feet might!

Of course, if you see the photographer at the ready and you know the horse at the in-gate is a notorious quitter, you might tip him off so he'll get set for a more spectacular picture—one that'll please the photo editor, the readers, and everyone—except for the owner and rider of the quitting horse!

If the paper is going to send a reporter, be sure he enjoys himself. He's working, certainly, but if he has a clean, reserved, well-located chair and table, an occasional cup of coffee from the refreshment tent (gratis, naturally), and a nearby expert to answer any questions, he might be so happy he'll write a happy story, thus attracting more customers the next day.

For many years, the only "A"-rated show in Buffalo was "poison" to sportswriters. They worked a seven-hour shift. When they came to the show at 7 P.M. they had to spend the first two or three hours typing up the morning and afternoon results! They were so busy with routine work they never had time to think of an interesting angle for the "lead" of their stories. If nothing else, have your secretary type up results after each class and make two or three carbon copies. Give a writer a chance to create, not labor!

If the newspaper cannot send a reporter the best thing the show committee can do, again, is hire its reporter-friend, the one who wrote those advance stories. He'll know the newspapers' deadlines (what time they must have the information they need), whether the newspapers plan to use just the winners of the classes, or first through fourth places, and so on.

He will also need someone to help him gather his information, or bring him to where the winner of the jumper class is stabled so the rider can give him details about the horse and some appropriate comments about the victory. A regular show rider who is injured or not competing usually serves this purpose very well.

If the television cameras come by to take film of the show, the station generally expects a telephone call later on with a quick summary of the show—"Rodney Jenkins won five classes and Buddy Brown won four"—or the winner of the day's featured class, or the class that was filmed. Be dependable, or you may never see the television cameras again.

Once the show is over everyone can relax except the publicity chairman. It's a nice touch to write a "thank you" letter to all the sports editors, reporters, and television newsmen who cooperated before and during the show. You want them to remember you favorably for next year's show, don't you?

18 Your Riding Future: Amateur or Professional?

You've always dreamed of it. Someone approaches you after you come out of a ring with a ribbon, or asks you to ride a strange horse at a show, or to come to their stable to work a difficult horse. And the dream ends with words like "You ride awfully well. Have you ever considered becoming a professional?"

The change from riding horses for fun to riding for a living is a big one. Of course it means the end of those dreams of Olympic Gold Medals, because only amateurs are eligible for Olympic and Pan American Games teams (in the United States, at any rate; other nations seem to have looser definitions of amateurism when it comes to its equestrians).

Riding other people's horses means new responsibilities, new challenges, and new dangers. But there is more to being a professional horseman than simply being an excellent rider.

There really is not that much of a decision to make, most young professional horsemen contend, because unless you come from a wealthy family and can afford to go down the show ring trail with one or two horses of your own, or have an extremely well-paying job that enables you to afford a horse or horses and enough nonworking time to ride regularly, the only way you can stay with the sport you love is to make it your profession. That is, if you're really devoted enough to put up with long hours, modest pay, pressure to achieve, and the many other duties that go with being a professional horseman.

From the stable operator's viewpoint, the young professional horseman is seen in a different light. John Shaffner asserts, "I can't afford someone who rides and does nothing else. Very few

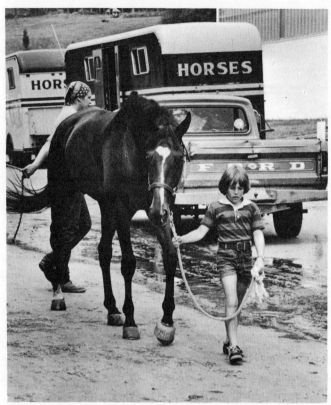

Addiction to the horse show world can begin at an early age. *Photo by Sue Maynard.*

operations can. But if a young rider has the ability, he'll ride more and more, you'll use his other talents. If someone really wants to be a top rider, and will stick with you and work hard, they'll make it."

When John married pretty, blonde Debby Hecht in 1972, many of his friends thought he had solved his problem of finding a top rider, so he could spend more time "on the ground" with the other aspects of running a show stable. After all, hadn't Debbie ridden the top show hunter Spindletop Please Note as a teenager, and ridden him well enough to have the horse bring a then-record price for a show hunter, a reported $40,000? Hadn't John asked her to ride professionally for him a year before they became engaged? And hadn't she also helped operate her father's stable in Syracuse for several years?

Suprisingly, the decision wasn't that simple. "I wanted to turn professional when John asked me," Debbie explained, "but then my father died and I had to stay near home until everything got back to normal. And although I'd ridden a lot as a teenager, most of the horses I was riding and showing—like Sun Imp, Shady Brook, Without Warning, Air Exec, Viscount, Belvoir, and Strawberry Hill—were 'made' horses, I'd had very little experience with green horses.

"I was riding three or four horses a day, but I really wasn't getting much instruction. Ted Roulston was a fine horseman, but he was preparing to retire and really hadn't been following newer methods of schooling and equitation. I really didn't have the experience to be a professional rider, to put it all together.

"First, John bought me Chili Multi (a handsome, blaze-faced chestnut), a really high-class horse. He began working with me, really giving me some rigid schooling. Having the advantage of a

After a while, you really enjoy being around horses all the time. (Kris Eberlein and Market Rise.) *Courtesy t. h. e. Studio; photo by Ken Schmidt.*

245

A professional horseman spends many hours alone with his students in an indoor arena. Ed Lane instructing at Hurdle Hill Farm. *Courtesy t. h. e. Studio; photo by Ken Schmidt.*

big indoor ring allowed me to continue working every day. Once I learned to ride Chili really well, I went on to other horses.

"But probably the one factor that kept me from becoming a professional immediately was that I didn't want to teach others to ride. And that is a necessity for most professional horsemen. Turning 'pro' depends on the individual situation, I believe. If you are single and have ridden a lot, there's more advantage to being a professional. But you have to be selective. You have to work for a good professional who can improve your riding and your reputation as a rider.

"Obviously, if you could keep one or two horses on the show circuit you can concentrate on riding them only, and you should win more and make a name for yourself. If you're a professional, you're expected to be able to ride anyone's horse and win on it.

"On the other hand, if you're a top pro and have two or three horses in a class, you certainly ought to learn how to ride the course properly and place at least one of your horses in the ribbons."

Diane Dubuc, a French-Canadian rider, is a licensed ski instructor and could earn enough in the winters to keep a show horse or two on the circuit each summer, but decided she would rather be a professional rider than ski instructor. "To make horses your living, you have to ride a lot of different ones, and being a professional is the only way to get that experience," she declared. "Before you can own a place of your own you have to learn about going to the bigger shows, stable management, business operations, and many other things."

Carol Shepherd, a native of Rochester, New York, who had begun working with green Thoroughbreds off the racetrack at fifteen, found her opportunity arising after two years of majoring in a college secretarial course. "Jack Frohm, owner of High View Farm, where I'd been keeping my horse, offered me a job," she recalled. "It was either being a secretary or being a horseman, and I thought I'd enjoy a stable more than an office.

Knowing how to operate farm machinery is important for a professional horseman or horsewoman. *Courtesy t. h. e. Studio; photo by Ken Schmidt.*

247

The horse's welfare always comes first. Leather Goods and Kate Bradley both may be hot, but he gets the shower first. *Courtesy t. h. e. Studio; photo by Ken Schmidt.*

"At first it wasn't much of a change, just getting paid for what I'd been doing for 'fun'—but more of it. In addition to the riding there was teaching, braiding, cleaning tack, cleaning horses, bandaging legs, clipping. But I've been doing it for some years now, and I don't regret it."

Carol's work day begins at 8 or 9 A.M. and ends at 6 P.M., usually. She rides about six horses a day, but "I could ride twenty if it wasn't for tacking them up first and cooling them out afterwards." Of course, continued work with young former race horses leads to a few bumps and bruises and sometimes more serious injuries.

"I once had a concussion and wound up with several stitches," she recalled. "I should have been using a protective helmet, but I wasn't. I still feel most hard riding hats are uncomfortable, and still don't use one unless I'm showing. A hard head is an asset for a horsewoman," she laughed.

A couple of years ago, another Rochester area horseman, Roger Young, was hurt in a fall and he, too, decided it was about time to stay on the ground and find a young rider to show his horses. Carol got the job.

"It was a good opportunity for me, but it meant more shows," Carol added. "For shows that are twenty to thirty miles away it means getting up at 4:30 A.M., being at the barn at 5 A.M., packing trunks and equipment, leaving at 6 A.M., getting to the show around 8 or 8:30, doing some schooling, and showing. Then it's arrive back at the stable anywhere from 9 P.M. to midnight, unpacking, checking over the horses, and then home to bed. We're showing nearly every week during the spring and summer. In the fall and winter there's almost one schooling show each week, which is an ideal time to get the young stock started."

Carol finds it no problem to own a horse of her own while riding other show horses. Her own horses have included such ribbon-winners as Shadow Lake, Quo Warranto, and Bound To Be, while the best-known horses she has ridden for Roger Young include Roman Talk and Tinker Toy. You don't spend that much time with each horse, she adds, so there is rarely a problem of an

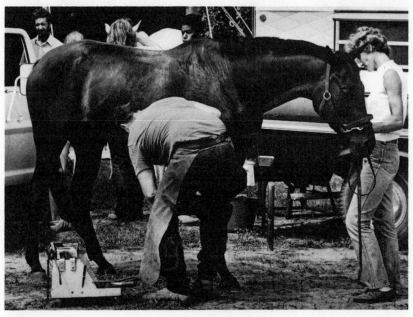

Only occasionally does a horse show groom get a chance to stand around and watch someone else work. *Photo by Sue Maynard.*

employer accusing you of neglecting his horses, or those of his customers, and spending too much time with your own horse.

Carol is paid $115 per week, but there are frequent bonuses, she emphasizes. "If I start a green horse and spend a lot of time riding and showing him, I get a commission when he is sold," she relates. "On the other hand, we may get a 'broke' child's horse in to sell and I may just ride him once or twice before he's bought, so I get no commission.

"If you go to a show and are asked to 'catch-ride' someone else's horse you're usually paid $10 for a round, more if you do well. Many horse-owners also give you extra payment when you do well at a show with their horse. It's not a really high-paying job, but I live at home and that cuts down on my living expenses. Of course, riding clothes are a big expense. I own four pairs of boots and probably five complete riding habits."

Carol doesn't believe every good amateur rider can become a professional rider. Most of them do not ride well enough, and so should limit riding to a hobby. "I don't think I could be satisfied doing that, unless I had a really interesting job to fill my nonriding time," she contends.

Most of the time, the horse show groom is on the move. *Photo by Sue Maynard.*

Although admitting she still gets "keyed up" at a big show like Devon, Pennsylvania, or Madison Square Garden, Carol finds the small schooling shows actually are the hardest because "You're riding the green ones, and you can't be sure what they might do. When it comes to work with green colts, it's a continuous process of discovery. Some horses look like great prospects during their first two weeks of training, and then take a turn for the worse. Others don't learn as fast and the rider is ready to think they'll never learn to jump a fence—then all at once they catch on to what they're supposed to do.

"Of course," says Carol, "you hope every young horse you start out will become a champion. The more championships he wins, the more he brings when you sell him, and the happier everyone is. When you work with so many horses, it is very easy to get into bad habits. That's why you can't go into business for yourself too quickly, you need the help of someone on the ground. Some tactic might work with one horse and not with another. Some horses jump better if you ride them close to the base of the fence, others might need to leave the ground at a longer distance.

"It's easy to get into the habit of riding all horses the same way. Sometimes you might think one should be ridden a certain way, but you're wrong. That's why I like to go to shows. You can get bored—and the horses can, too—going over the same fences in the same ring over and over again. And you get tired of seeing the same people day after day."

Carol Shepherd says the least enjoyable tasks she has are driving all night to get to a show, and having to be responsible for thirteen and fourteen year olds. "I have to drive them back and forth, from the motel to the show and elsewhere, and they just get on my nerves. Children that age seem to be continually laughing, screaming, and carrying on. Six or seven of them around you constantly is enough to drive you crazy."

For those young riders thinking about becoming professionals, Carol urges "spending as much time as you can with your own horse or at the stable where he's kept, if you don't have him at home. Learn to clean tack, braid manes and tails, and do other stable chores. The more time you spend around a barn, the more you'll learn."

Debbie Deutl, a native of Schenectady, New York, comes from a "pro" family. Her sister, Diane, worked for former USET rider George Morris, now one of the nation's leading instructors, and

A groom is responsible not only for the horses, but also for tack and other equipment. *Photo by Sue Maynard.*

now owns her own Bucks Mill Farm in Bucks County, Pennsylvania. Her brother, David, with some other friends, organized "Blue Ribbon Braiding," going to shows and working all night braiding manes and tails for five dollars when most free-lance grooms were charging ten dollars. He now is involved in horse show management.

Debbie had her first horse at thirteen, a junior jumper, The Orbiter, and later showed her sister's horse, Carry On, when spending summers as a working pupil with Morris, and, later, Wayne Carroll. During the school year she helped at a small stable at home, "training a little and getting some money off my board bill." Later she worked as a summer groom for top professionals Carl Knee and Henry Hulick. She enrolled at Lake Erie College as a freshman in 1972 and moved her horse, Second Nature, to the nearby stable of Lutz Andahazy.

"I did some instructing and rode other horses, went to shows, and somehow kept from flunking out of college," she related. "But horses were too interesting; once you're hooked on them, you're with them to stay. Once the school year was over I went to shows all summer. I groomed, rode, braided, and began giving more lessons.

252

"The biggest change I noted after turning professional was being responsible to the owners of the different horses. You had to answer to the trainer, Lutz, and also to the owners. Some wanted their horses to be the best at every show, and they really made you feel the pressure. Other owners were more understanding when you made a mistake or the horse made one.

"Teaching wasn't that new an experience. The little ones, nine to fourteen years, were fine. I had observed the teaching techniques of the professionals I'd worked with and adopted my own style. Students my own age respected me for my riding ability. Adults were a little different. But after a while they forgot about my age and listened to what I had to offer them. No professional can ever just ride and go to a show to show his own horses. You must develop other riders so they can show. Their showing horses makes it possible for you to afford to show your own stock."

According to Debbie, becoming a professional horseman "involves a lot of listening so you can learn about running a business,

A blue ribbon hanging from your pocket makes you feel a little happier as you rub down a top show hunter like Another Legend. *Photo by Sue Maynard.*

253

Homeward bound at last, but with a mountain of tack to be cleaned for the next show. *Photo by Sue Maynard.*

buying and selling, teaching. You just have to sort out a lot of things to decide what will work best. As for your own riding, as you become more mature in age and attitude your own riding form becomes more mature. Most professionals teach a uniform style, with only a few modifications. Learning to ride better is just a part of growing up, I think. You learn to modify your own opinion and attitudes—about proper form in the saddle and everything else. You just have to grow up!"

Many of Debbie's riding friends at home now have stopped riding. Others she has shown with did not remain involved with horses. Some rode well and were ribbon winners but, she believes, "didn't have the real, true feeling for horses that makes up for the long, hard road of being a professional. It takes a lot of stamina. The hours are long. You can get run down. Sometimes I don't feel I'm a woman, just a machine—but a couple of days of the proper amount of rest and you are ready to go again."

254

19 Your Riding Future:
Colleges of Equestrian Knowledge

But what do you do if you've never been able to own your own horse, or take lessons from a top trainer, or show a horse on a major show circuit—and still want to become a professional horseman?

There can be little doubt that the huge increase in the numbers of pleasure and show horses in every section of North America is creating new jobs. Twenty or thirty years ago the source of supply was the American or European cavalry schools, or the professional groom from England or Ireland. Now these sources are virtually nonexistent.

How many parents have heard these words from their horse-crazy boy or girl aged 18? "Mom, Dad, guess what? Joe Pro says I can work for him! And after I get up at 6 A.M. to feed, muck out fifteen stalls, groom, polish tack, and teach a few lessons, I can ride as much as I want to!"

Working with horses does involve long hours, much purely physical labor and—in most cases—living on the stable property. Having one's child live away from home may be the most serious objection a parent can have, and understandably so.

There also is little doubt that many professional horsemen look upon the legions of horse-loving youngsters as a source of cheap labor. For many of these youngsters their first, or first few, jobs will qualify them for little more than a "degree" in cleaning out stalls.

One of the best solutions to the problem is the growing numbers of riding schools and colleges that have developed programs to prepare young people for employment in the

The first thing a prospective professional horseman must learn is to ride well himself. This class is drilling at the Pacific Horse Center in California.

wonderful world of horses. They solve many problems for anxious parents: they keep the youngster out of the labor market for a few months or years, thus giving him more time to mature; they get the youngster away from home (possibly for the first time), but he is with others in the same situation, so the adjustment is easier; he is being prepared with a marketable skill; he is proving his interest in the field to prospective employers by investing time and money learning necessary skills; and he gets an opportunity to travel, broadening his education in still another direction.

For the student who is not sure about his future and who has been a good student in high school, the four-year college with a strong program in riding may be the answer. Should he discover that other fields can be just as exciting and interesting as horses—and require more normal working hours and offer more opportunity for advancement—his time has been well-spent.

Let's look over a few of these programs, inspect what they have to offer, and some of the philosophies behind them.

Morven Park International Equestrian Institute in Leesburg, Virginia, probably boasted the most famous director/chief instructor in the late Maj. John Lynch, who had trained the U.S. Equestrian Team's Three-Day Event team and several world-famous eventing horses.

Morven Park aims at eliminating the one criticism that many professional horsemen make of many riding school graduates—that they do not ride well enough. Morven Park's object is "first to teach people to ride correctly and school horses; then, after they have been thoroughly taught to teach themselves, to teach others." Maj. Lynch continued:

"All the military equitation schools of note in the world always were twelve months. (Morven Park's program began at nine months, now it's eleven.) And one had to be well qualified before acceptance, at the regimental level commanding a troop of about fifty horses. In England, this meant you had probably hunted since childhood and while serving in India, Egypt, and other parts of the British Empire, had played polo, raced, and gone pig-sticking. Those instructors had a lifetime with horses before taking the course.

But you also have to be able to teach the principles of riding to pupils of all ages, in a class or on a one-to-one basis on the longe line, as shown here at 5 H Acres School of Horsemanship, Cortland, New York.

"Although it takes less and less time in the world to get from one place to another, it still takes the same amount of time that it did fifty years ago to teach a person to ride and teach a person to teach. It takes the same length of time to train a horse that it did in our grandfathers' day, although the technique may be a little better."

Maj. Lynch felt Morven Park students must be at least at Pony Club B level before enrolling and be prepared "to think, live and breathe horses for the eleven months you are here. What we are noted for, and what all military riding schools were noted for, is producing an articulate instructor with clear-cut aims and ideals, and poise and character enough to take command—and I emphasize command—of whatever class they intend to teach."

In addition to riding, training, and teaching riding, instruction also includes the economics of running a riding school from the business side, and a veterinary program. Tuition, excluding room and board, for the equitation instructor course, is $4,828 (as of 1978). Room and board is an additional $2,530. During the summer Morven Park offers a three-week course (tuition $500) in equitation, stable management, and equine first aid and veterinary care.

A Morven Park student shows fine form over a jump in one of the institute's two indoor arenas.

258

Newly into a horsemanship program is Virginia Intermont College, Bristol, Virginia, which first expanded from a junior (two-year) college to a four-year institution. Its two-year Assistant Instructor's Certificate likewise expanded into a four-year Bachelor of Arts degree in Horsemanship.

Mary Harrington, director of riding, notes the value of the four-year course as follows:

"First, it seems the better-paying jobs, more and more, are requiring a bachelor's degree. Our program is designed with a strong emphasis on a double major. Some are combining horsemanship with merchandising and psychology-sociology. The double major allows more flexibility in job selection. Many students have a specific job in mind related to the 'world of horses'; others are not sure they want to make horsemanship a career."

Students ride four hours weekly as freshmen, six hours as sophomores and six to ten hours as upperclassmen. Course work includes judging horse show classes, schooling, elementary dressage, teaching, stable management, fox hunting, recreational riding, combined training, participating in, organizing, and coaching riders for shows, and independent study; student teaching is "a minimum of 120 clock hours."

The Pacific Horse Center, Elk Grove, California, operates two complimentary courses leading to employment in the horse field. The "horsemastership course" of twelve weeks is designed for those who wish to improve their riding, to become assistant instructors, or for pleasure and personal satisfaction.

One must complete this course to take the "advanced horsemastership course," also of twelve weeks, to qualify for an instructor's diploma. Students in the program are assigned two horses: one to show and the other, a green horse, to care for and train under supervision. The two courses now are combined into one four-month course, with a cost of $2,800.

Lawrence Langer, director and owner, notes that he is working with a nearby junior college to put together a two-year degree program, explaining, "I feel such a program would be of extreme value to many students by giving them a more well-rounded education. It also would satisfy the many parents who are appalled at the thought of their children entering the work force without some more formal higher education. I can agree with these parents.

Morven Park students relax between riding session in the institute's cafeteria.

"However, I do not plan to give up the more intensive programs, because I feel they are the most economical way to learn. At the normal tuition and board rate of $250 per month in a California college, it would take about three years and $9,000 to learn as much as we teach in six months."

Mrs. Blanche Hendrickson, former owner of 5 H Acres School of Riding in Cortland, New York, believes the advantage of a formal instruction program over an apprenticeship is that "it is an organized sequence of study, and student-oriented. By examining the course outline and content the student should have a fair idea of what he will learn and how fast he will learn it.

"Since the school's products are successful students, he is entitled to expect that the school will be more concerned with him and his progress than if it were principally engaged in breeding, training, or boarding horses. For instance, most schools try to provide special educational experiences such as field trips, lectures, and clinics that would not normally be available to the apprentice. Most schools take an active role in placing their graduates in the right job. Most also offer educational aids—films, a library, charts, models—which may not be available elsewhere.

"More and more, employers are looking for applicants with

some systematic and recognized training in horsemanship, with the reputation of a good school to back them up."

At 5 H, the emphasis is on a small, select program—and part-time attendance at a nearby junior college. Students must take two courses each year, usually English, psychology, or public speaking, and a business course. Mrs. Hendrickson notes that a start of nine to twelve credits usually leads most students to complete two- or four-year degree programs.

The course covers two years. Tuition is $5,290 (in 1977) for one year, including room and board, and the emphasis is on instruction and stable management.

A former teacher, Mrs. Hendrickson is a strong advocate of the college-related riding instructor school, but would like to see them strengthened through a national organization that could set up minimum standards and certification. The American Camping Association may move into the area of camp riding instructor programs as it has done with the Red Cross Water Safety Instructor program.

What a riding school program offers that an apprenticeship does not are formal lectures.

A well-rounded horseman should be acquainted with Western riding (left) and also with the dressage ring (right).

Mrs. Hendrickson notes, however, that a career course is not the answer for everybody, "especially in the field of training, where individual talent and technique are so important and reputation is everything. Those who want to train show horses are better off apprenticing themselves to a good trainer. 'On-the-circuit' experience is invaluable and beyond the capabilities of most schools.

"However, not all good trainers like to—or can—teach young people. Those who can usually are swamped with applicants. And the greatest and most common error is to assume that experience in one area qualifies that person in another (a successful hunter equitation rider assumes he is automatically qualified to teach others)."

John Shaffner contends that "If a boy or girl has the proper attitude and a willingness to work, I'm willing to help him, as are many other professionals. He earns as he learns, too. It's harder than a school, no doubt about that, the hours are much longer. But at the end of two or three years I think they'll be further ahead as show trainers or show riders.

"In the school programs it seems the students braid a horse to learn how to braid. In my stable we braid a horse so he can look

right to win a ribbon. Here we bandage front legs to cure an ailment, not to learn how to bandage. Obviously, our grooms braid many more horses each week than anyone would do in a school program. The show stable does everything the school does—only more of it: more grooming, more braiding, more lessons, more transporting of horses.

"Most youngsters drop out of the business, because if they start as a groom it takes a long time to get to be a show rider. Most of them won't wait that long or work that hard in the meantime. But it's rare that a professional hires someone at the 'top'—as a rider only. It's better to start low and work up with the same man; if you keep moving from job to job you usually have to keep starting near the bottom each time."

Jack Frohm, who owns and operates High View Farm in Pittsford, New York, is one of a growing number of professional horsemen who are college graduates. Others in the East include George Morris, Victor Hugo-Vidal, Barney Ward, and Roger Young. Frohm combined studies at Cornell University with playing polo, teaching riding and training. He feels the experience broadened his outlook considerably.

"It made me realize that a stable is a business and, like any other commercial enterprise, must be operated as a business," he explained. "You realize there is more to running a stable than just

263

sitting in the saddle. Most people get into the horse business because they are good riders. But they learn that there is more to it than that. You must diversify to be successful: you must offer year-round riding lessons, perhaps a summer day camp, a polo league, horse shows, a tack shop. If one area hits a slump, the others may be doing better and balance it all out.

"If you are ever going to have a place of your own, you are going to have to deal with bankers. They definitely respect a college degree or some type of formal training. A stable is a big financial investment, since generally it must be near a highly populated area. This experience, by the way, has helped me develop a profitable sideline in real estate investment.

"As you go along, and your operation expands, you find you're more a businessman, more of a professional manager than a professional horseman. Although you get into the field because you're a good rider, you find you can't 'afford' to ride, you can't 'afford' the time. The cost of your land is high, your taxes are high, the cost of horses is high, you have employees' wages to pay, and you have to make the entire operation show a profit.

"You have to be mature enough to give up being the 'star' in the show ring. You can't insist that you can do everything better than anyone else. You must be able to delegate responsibility. Some of your employees should be able to do some things better than you can. If they can, then your business has that much more of a chance to be successful."

In view of Frohm's comments about the diversity of the modern large stable operation, the comments of riding program directors on the type of young people who make the most successful professional horsemen are both interesting and somewhat unexpected.

Ms. Harrington, at Virginia Intermont, states: "I do advise students as to whether they ride well enough to plan to go into schooling, or whether they can communicate and analyze student problems well enough to teach. I have had rank beginners who, by the end of four years, held down very good teaching jobs. And I have had very good riders who cannot teach."

Major Lynch notified Morven Park students if they did not measure up to standards midway through the course. They could either continue without the hope of graduating, unless there was drastic improvement, or leave. He pointed out:

"With the young instructors, there is a tendency to feel that

264

they should start at the top. This conceit one tries to eradicate before they leave. When they leave a school they only know the 'ten commandments of riding' and realize when they or their students are breaking them. How good they are going to be eventually depends on experience, enthusiasm, and dedication.

"The character and determination of every student being different, one gets some very pleasant surprises by finding that students well down the course (in teachers' ratings) are doing a very competent job and looked up to in their riding community.

"I think more than anything else the remarks from many parents on graduation day that their daughter or son has grown up, is more competent and assured, and that we have brought out the best traits in their offspring's character are the most satisfying. Apart from the equitation training, they are made to run a stable, give orders, make sure they are obeyed, and compete in instructing large numbers of people. After being exposed to this for nine months, even the most timid and hesitant change greatly before the end of the course."

Mr. Langer of the Pacific Horse Center believes that students

The late Maj. John Lynch, a former international level rider and coach, teaching a class at the Morven Park International Equestrian Institute in Leesburg, Virginia.

who come in with extensive equestrian backgrounds absorb the information much faster and can pursue worthwhile careers after six months. But, he continues:

"Other students come with relatively little background, still wanting to pursue a career with horses. Although their progress is astounding, they simply are not qualified to immediately work in the field and are told so. We suggest they either go to another trainer or another school for more instruction.

"We do not, however, ordinarily tell them that they cannot ever make it in the horse world, because there are many successful trainers and instructors whose original teachers never thought that they had talent. Through hard work and diligent effort they made it—and so could these others."

Mrs. Hendrickson emphasizes, "It is not enough to be a top or to know all the theory. In order to get and keep a top job, you must be able to handle people, whether they are clients or their parents, the public, your employers, or your employees. A great deal of the course is devoted to 'people' subjects—psychology and teaching methods for dealing with students; English and other subjects to give you the background and confidence to deal with the public; and public relations, advertising, and business practices that should keep the business going once you get it started.

"In teaching it is so important to give, and to be willing to put out extra effort for someone else. Occasionally we come across a student who is so concerned with himself and his own problems and achievements that he is unable to reach out to other people. We will try to help, but if he is unable or unwilling to work with people—rather than just horses—we cannot work with him.

"It is much easier for all concerned if we do not accept such a student in the first place. We are 'turned off' by applicants who start in by describing their show records and stress 'I,' 'me,' and 'my riding' too much. Attitude is especially important when it comes to being hired and keeping a job. Many people in the horse world drift from one job to another, with lots of talent and ability but without the maturity, self-discipline, and responsibility to make a worthwhile employee.

"Almost all young people interested in horses want to reach 'the top'—usually meaning success in showing at a high level. All too few have the real ability and dedication it takes to become one of the best in any form of riding. They have to learn to be

A Pacific Horse Center student takes a jump as the rest of his class observes.

realistic, especially in the type of job they seek. I would not discourage anyone from the pursuit of excellence, but it is possible to be carried away with ideas of fame, glory, and winning.

"As far as we are concerned, the instructor who introduces his students to the horse world, the trainer who starts a young horse, the breeder and the stable manager, and a thousand others can reach just as high a level in their own way as an Olympic champion—and may be even more important to the horse world."

Lawrence Langer goes even further, foreseeing the day when show jumping and other horse sports are televised nationally and internationally in prime viewing time, when professional riders compete on a regular circuit and earn more than $100,000 annually, when top horses command four or five times their present high prices, when riding is as popular as cycling, fishing, or boating, and when trainers are licensed by the industry or by the state. Then, as well as now, the properly trained horseman will be in demand in all facets of the horse industry.

Index